The Challenges of Mandating School Uniforms in the Public Schools

Also by Todd A. DeMitchell

Labor Relations in Education: Policies, Politics, and Practices
Negligence: What Principals Need to Know About Avoiding Liability

Also by Todd A. DeMitchell and Richard Fossey

The Limits of Law-Based School Reform
Student Dress Codes and the First Amendment: Legal Challenges and Policy Issues

The Challenges of Mandating School Uniforms in the Public Schools

Free Speech, Research, and Policy

Todd A. DeMitchell and Richard Fossey

ROWMAN & LITTLEFIELD
Lanham • Boulder • New York • London

Published by Rowman & Littlefield
A wholly owned subsidiary of The Rowman & Littlefield Publishing Group, Inc.
4501 Forbes Boulevard, Suite 200, Lanham, Maryland 20706
www.rowman.com

Unit A, Whitacre Mews, 26-34 Stannary Street, London SE11 4AB

British Library Cataloguing in Publication Information Available

Library of Congress Cataloging-in-Publication Data
DeMitchell, Todd A., author.
The challenges of mandating school uniforms in the public schools : free speech, research, and policy / Todd A. DeMitchell, Richard Fossey.
pages cm
ISBN 978-1-4758-0933-6 (hardcover) — ISBN 978-1-4758-0934-3 (pbk.) — ISBN 978-1-4758-0935-0 (e-book) 1. Students—United States—Uniforms. 2. Freedom of expression—United States. 3. Dress codes in schools (2014) 4. Dress codes—Law and legislation—United States. 5. Students—Clothing—United States. 6. Students—Civil rights—United States. 7. Students—Legal status, laws, etc.—United States. I. Fossey, Richard, author. II. Title.
KF4770.D47 2015
344.73'0793—dc23 2015013274

∞ ™ The paper used in this publication meets the minimum requirements of American National Standard for Information Sciences Permanence of Paper for Printed Library Materials, ANSI/NISO Z39.48-1992.

Printed in the United States of America

We gratefully acknowledge and deeply appreciate the support that our wives, Terri (Todd) and Kim (Richard), have unstintingly given to us, and we, with gratitude, thank them.

Contents

Preface

Are school uniforms a real remedy for the thorny problems that beset our public schools or are they just a placebo that masks the heavy lifting that real achievement and school cultural change require? [1]

WHY WRITE THIS BOOK?

This book and its companion volume, *Student Dress Codes and the First Amendment: Legal Challenges and Policy Issues*,[2] explore what students are prohibited from wearing to school and what they must wear to school. Together these two books examine the two primary battlegrounds of litigation over student attire: dress codes that *prohibit* certain types of clothing from being worn to school, and school-uniform policies that dictate what students *must* wear to school. For good or for ill, a student's mundane morning decision about what to wear to school is often dressed in constitutional garb.

In recent years, students and their parents have filed lawsuits challenging school districts' restrictions on what can be worn at school and what must be worn at school. These lawsuits highlight the conflict between the constitutional right of students to express themselves in the clothes they wear to school with the school's interest in providing a safe and orderly learning environment. These conflicts have generated a surprising amount of litigation on the constitutional dimensions of what students wear to school, and this litigation has forced school districts to expend precious time and money to defend their polices on student dress—time and money that would be better spent on student instruction.

For example, Dreaming Bear, a Native American student in South Dakota, wanted to wear his traditional Lakota clothing rather than the standard cap and gown at his graduation ceremony. When his request was denied, he brought a federal lawsuit.[3] A New Mexico student brought suit asserting that he had an expressive-speech right to wear sagging pants to school.[4] A Nevada high-school student argued that the school's mandatory school-uniform policy prevented her from engaging in pure speech. In the student's view, the school uniform of solid khaki-colored bottoms and solid-colored shirts compelled her to speak in a particular manner.[5] And students have brought suit seeking to wear "I ♥ Boobies (Keep a Breast)" bracelets that support breast cancer awareness.[6]

The issue presented to the courts in these lawsuits is whether public schools infringe on the free-expression rights of students when they prohibit students from wearing certain articles or types of clothing or require students to wear a uniform to school. Most often the controversy surrounding student appearance litigation "is a tale without heroes and without villains."[7]

Recent events in Goldendale School District (State of Washington) illustrate the balance that educators, parents, and community seek between the rights of students and the selection of the best policy approach (dress code or school uniform) for establishing and maintaining a proper educational environment for students. The school board's community meeting on February 13, 2013 in the Goldendale High School cafeteria centered on whether high-school students should wear school uniforms.[8] The high school had a dress-code policy but was considering a uniform look for its students.

School-uniform advocates argued that school uniforms would cut down on the time that school personnel spent in handling dress-code violations, which involved about 15 percent of the students. But one attendee questioned this logic, stating that if students were violating the dress code, "why don't we do more of the enforcement things?"[9] Another individual stated that a lot of parents who were poor were concerned about the cost of school uniforms because they would still need to buy clothes for their children to wear outside of school. One parent asked that more data and less anecdotal evidence be provided: "I could go either way, but I want data."[10]

Five students from the Goldendale High School Leadership class spoke at the meeting. They raised a cautionary flag about the school-uniform policy. The students told the assembly of parents, community members, and educators that they were willing "to do better not to go to a uniform."[11] One of the students said, "I am definitely emotional about this. These are things I take personally."[12]

In June, the school board concluded the year without making a decision about whether to adopt a school-uniform policy: "the board is still trying to figure it out."[13] One school board member expressed the view that the school district would be better off enforcing the dress code that was currently in place rather than instituting a school-uniform policy.[14]

In the end, Goldendale's school board decided to stay with the status quo. Apparently, the board agreed with the board member who argued for better enforcement of the current student dress code rather than adopting a controversial school-uniform policy.

The policy debate in the Goldendale School District encapsulates much of the national discussion about the wisdom of mandating school uniforms in public schools. In the end, two prominent questions are raised every time school authorities contemplate the adoption of a mandatory school-uniform policy for students: First, does the research support the claims of school-uniform proponents that school uniforms will improve academic performance and school discipline? Second, will the courts uphold school districts' school-uniform polices if they are challenged on constitutional grounds?

SEEKING THE CORRECT BALANCE: RIGHTS AND RESPONSIBILITIES

The ongoing controversy about regulating what students wear to school reflects an important tension in public education. On one hand, public schools must protect the constitutional rights of their students. On the other hand, the school acts *in loco parentis* to students and must provide them with a safe learning environment.[15] As one federal court observed, "Courts have long struggled to balance the First Amendment rights of students with the need of school administrators to maintain a safe and educational environment in our nation's schools."[16] Often there is a conflict between these two responsibilities that student clothing brings into sharp focus.

Freedom of speech, in any context, is not absolute.[17] As the Supreme Court observed in *Cornelius v. NAACP*:

> Even protected speech is not equally permissible in all places and at all times. Nothing in the Constitution requires the government freely to grant access to all who wish to exercise their right to free speech on every type of Government

> property without regard to the nature of the property or to the disruption that might be caused by the speaker's activities.[18]

Public schools are one type of government property where free speech can sometimes be restricted. As Chief Justice Burger asserted in *Bethel School District No. 403 v. Fraser*, "The constitutional rights of students in public school are not automatically coextensive with the rights of adults in other settings."[19] Clearly some forms of expression allowed by adults may be prohibited to children in a public school.

A school is generally considered a nonpublic forum for purposes of the First Amendment; therefore, the state can exercise a greater degree of control than it could if schools were an open forum.[20] The courts have reduced student First Amendment rights by giving deference to school administrators' judgment as to what speech is appropriate in the context of the public school.[21] In *Hazelwood School District v. Kuhlmeier*, the US Supreme Court opined, "We thus recognized that the determination of what manner of speech in the classroom or in school assembly is appropriate properly rests with the school board rather than the federal courts."[22] For example, in a T-shirt case in Massachusetts, a federal court judge opined, "At least in high school, a political message does not justify a vulgar medium."[23]

Clearly, school officials and students do not always share the same opinion of what is appropriate to wear to school. But if a school chooses to adopt a specific policy that restricts what students may wear to school, that policy must comport with established and guaranteed constitutional freedoms.[24]

THE ORGANIZATION OF THE BOOK

The push to expand individual freedoms in our public schools must be balanced against the legitimate interest of the state in educating its citizenry. Students have the right to freedom of expression at school, but school authorities have a compelling state interest in having public schools run in an efficient manner. Dress codes and school-uniform policies reflect the tension between individual rights and institutional responsibilities in the school setting. The implementation of a dress code or a mandatory uniform policy has not been without controversy. Students who challenge dress codes typically assert that the dress code infringes on their right to freedom of expression, and they often argue that a particular dress code is unconstitutionally vague or overbroad. However, a middle-school principal suggested that school uniforms may be the appropriate remedy for students who are "'draggin,' 'saggin,' and 'laggin.'"[25]

"What students wear has become a major issue in the nation's schools."[26] A 2014 *New York Times* op-ed piece titled "The Battle Over Dress Codes"[27] posited that what students wear to school should essentially be the family's call. Peggy Ornstein, an op-ed contributor, argued that dress code should adopt the following:

> Clothing must allow students a full range of motion—sitting, bending, reaching, running—without requiring perpetual readjustment. It cannot, in other words, pose a "distraction" to the wearer.[28]

Adding to the controversy of whether the regulation of student dress is constitutional, the op-ed writer is concerned that dress codes unfairly target female students.[29]

A considerable body of educational, policy, and legal commentary has been devoted to this topic. Schools have reached different conclusions about whether to regulate student clothing. Some have adopted stringent dress codes, some have implemented school-uniform policies, and some have decided not to regulate student dress at all beyond maintaining minimum standards for modesty and cleanliness.

The book is organized into six chapters. The first chapter, "School Uniforms and Dress Codes: From the Clothes Closet to the Courtroom," explains the difference between dress codes and school uniforms. Chapter 2, entitled "Student Free Speech and Clothing Choices," explores the constitutional foundation for most dress-code and school-uniform cases. In this chapter, the US Supreme Court's four major student free-speech cases are discussed: *Tinker v. Des Moines Independent Community School District, (Tinker)*;[30] *Bethel School District No. 403 v. Fraser, (Fraser)*;[31] *Hazelwood School District v. Kuhlmeier, (Kuhlmeier)*;[32] and *Morse v. Frederick, (Morse)*.[33]

Because there has been an emerging trend, especially in school-uniform cases, to use noneducation cases as the basis for the courts' legal analysis, cases such as *Texas v. Johnson*,[34] *Spence v. Washington*,[35] and *United States v. O'Brien*[36] are discussed in chapter 3, which is entitled "Draft Cards and the American Flag: Noneducation Free-Speech Cases." Chapters 2 and 3 form the legal foundation for the rest of the book's exploration of student-attire policies.

Chapter 4, "School Uniforms: Required Attire," focuses the discussion on school-uniform litigation. This chapter analyzes the school-uniform cases chronologically, starting with a 1997 decision out of Arizona[37] and concluding with the Ninth Circuit's 2014 decision in *Frudden v. Pilling*.[38] This chapter analyzes the facts and legal reasoning of all the published court opinions involving challenges to school-uniform policies.

The fifth chapter, "Research on School Uniforms: Mixed Results," reviews the research literature on the effectiveness of school-uniform policies as a strategy for improving academic achievement and maintaining school discipline. As this chapter explains, the research findings are mixed regarding the effectiveness of school uniforms as a means of improving the school environment.

The last chapter, "Policy Implications for Dress Codes and School Uniforms: Balancing Rights and Responsibilities" discusses the policy implications on dress codes and mandatory school uniforms in the nation's public schools. The legal ramifications and research implications of these policies are explored. The book is limited to a study of student attire focusing on school uniforms. While school policies on student grooming (hair length for example) are sometimes litigated in the courts, these legal disputes are beyond the scope of this book.

Dress codes and mandatory uniforms have not resolved the age-old question of what should students wear to school. In an interesting twist, St. Paul's School (a private school) in Concord, New Hampshire, added blue jeans to the dress code as acceptable student attire. Some students were outraged and worried that "the addition of blue jeans to the dress code would make our school appear sloppy and less put together." Other students "relished this new opportunity, enjoying the fact that it would be easier to get ready in the morning."[39] In a poll of 150 male and female students, "more boys than girls said that they never wore jeans to classes and gave some of the strongest arguments against the new dress code."[40] Apparently, not even students can agree on what they should be allowed to wear to school.

From our early research on dress codes and school uniforms with our colleague Casey Cobb, we are reminded of the responses from two principals about the value of dress codes. One succinctly wrote, "Proper Dress = Success," and one rural principal opined, "Some would come Nude without it."[41] It is our hope that this book will provide a useful guide for educators, researchers, and parents as they address the constitutional implications of school-uniform policies along with the current research on the effectiveness of such policies as a means of improving the learning environment in our nation's schools.

NOTES

1. Todd A. DeMitchell, "School Uniforms: There Is No Free Lunch," *Teachers College Record*, December 14, 2006, ID 12891, http://www.tcrecord.org/content.asp?contentid=12891.

2. Richard Fossey and Todd A. DeMitchell, *Student Dress Codes and the First Amendment: Legal Challenges and Policy Issues* (Lanham, MD: Rowman & Littlefield, 2014). The dress-code litigation was organized into three chapters: "Dress Codes: Pants, Hats, and Gangs—The Clothes Are the Message" (chapter 3); "Drugs, Politics, and the Confederate Battle Flag: Targeted Messages on Students' Clothing" (chapter 4); and "Clothing Messages about Sex, Abortion, and Sexual Orientation" (chapter 5).

3. Bear v. Fleming, 714 F. Supp. 2d 972 (D.S.D. 2010).

4. Bivens v. Albuquerque Public Schools, 899 F. Supp. 556 (D.N.M. 1995).

5. Jacobs v. Clark County School District, 526 F.3d 419, 426 (9th Cir. 2008).

6. K.J. v. Sauk Prairie School District, 11-cv-622-bbc, 2012 U.S. Dis. LEXIS 187689 (W.D. Wis. 2012) but B.H. v. Easton Area School District, 725 F.3d 293 (3d Cir. 2013) found the ban unconstitutional.

7. Pyle By and Through Pyle v. South Hadley School Committee, 861 F. Supp. 157, 173 (D. Mass 1994).

8. Deb Brumley, "School Meeting Opens Discussion on School Uniforms, Budget Issues," *Goldendale Sentinel* (Goldendale, WA), February 13, 2013, http://www.goldendalesentinel.com/story/2013/02/13/news/school-meeting-opens-discussion-on-school-uniforms-budget-issues/2105.html.

9. Ibid.

10. Ibid.

11. Ibid.

12. Ibid.

13. Deb Brumley, "School Meeting Sheds New Light on Uniforms, Restaffing," *Goldendale Sentinel* (Goldendale, WA), June 12, 2013, http://www.goldendalesentinel.com/story/2013/06/12/news/school-meeting-sheds-new-light-on-uniforms-restaffing/2682.html.

14. In support, a parent at the school board meeting stated that enforcing the current dress code is more important than changing the dress code to a school uniform. Ibid.

15. See Todd A. DeMitchell, *Negligence: What Principals Need to Know About Avoiding Liability* (Lanham, MD: Rowman & Littlefield Education, 2006); Todd A. DeMitchell, "The Duty to Protect: Blackstone's Doctrine of *In Loco Parentis*. A Lens for Viewing the Sexual Abuse of Students," *Brigham Young University Education and Law Journal* (2002): 17.

16. Dariano v. Morgan Hill Unified School District, 822 F. Supp. 2d 1037, 1042 (N.D. Cal. 2011). See also LaVine v. Blaine School District, 257 F.3d 981, 992 (9th Cir. 2001), balancing the critical importance of establishing and maintaining a safe school environment by giving deference to "schools' decisions in connection with the safety of their students even when freedom of expression is involved."

17. Whitney v. California, 274 U.S. 357, 373 (1927) ("[A]lthough the rights of free speech and assembly are fundamental, they are not in their nature absolute.).

18. 473 U.S. 788, 799-800 (1985).

19. Bethel School District No. 403 v. Fraser, 478 U.S. 675, 682 (1986).

20. See, for example, Lamb's Chapel v. Center Moriches Free School District, 508 U.S. 384 (1993); Hazelwood School District v. Kuhlmeier, 484 U.S. 260 (1988). For a discussion of fora in public educational settings, see Perry Educational Association v. Perry Local Educator's Association, 460 U.S. 37 (1983).

21. Denno v. School Board of Volusia County, 959 F. Supp. 1481 (M.D. Fla. 1997).

22. Hazelwood School District v. Kuhlmeier, 484 U.S. at 267 (1988).

23. Pyle By and Through Pyle v. South Hadley School Committee, 861 F. Supp. 157, 169 (D. Mass 1994).

24. See West Virginia State Board of Education v. Barnette, 319 U.S. 624, 637 (1943) ("The Fourteenth Amendment, as now applied to the States, protects the citizen against the State itself and all of its creatures—Boards of Education not excepted. These have, of course, important, delicate, and highly discretionary functions, but none that they may not perform within the limits of the Bill of Rights.").

25. United States Department of Education, *Manual of School Uniforms*, (n.d.), available at http://www.ed.gov/updates/uniforms.html.

26. Christopher B. Gilbert. "We Are What We Wear: Revisiting Student Dress Codes," *Brigham Young University Education and Law Journal* (1999): 3. See also "Uniforms Suddenly a Hot Topic: Can Students Dress for Success?" *School Violence Alert* 2, no. 4 (April 1996); Keith A. King, "Should School Uniforms be Mandated in Elementary Schools?" *Journal of School Health* 68 (1998): 32; Troy Y. Nelson, "If Clothes Make the Person, Do Uniforms Make the Student? Constitutional Free Speech Rights and Student Uniforms," *Education Law Reporter* 118 (1997): 1; and American Civil Liberties Union of Massachusetts, News Release, *All This in the Name of Order*, available at http://users.aol.com/mcluf/lawr.htm.

27. Peggy Orenstein, "The Battle Over Dress Codes," *New York Times*, June 13, 2014, http://www.nytimes.com/2014/06/14/opinion/the-battle-over-dress-codes.html?_r=0.

28. Ibid.

29. She writes, "Girls, particularly those with ample hips or breasts, are most exclusively singled out, typically told their outfits will 'distract boys.' As if young men cannot control themselves in the presence of a spaghetti strap." Ibid.

30. Tinker v. Des Moines Independent Community School District, 393 U.S. 503 (1969).

31. Bethel School District No. 403 v. Fraser, 478 U.S. 675 (1986).

32. Hazelwood School District. v. Kuhlmeier, 484 U.S. 260 (1988).

33. Morse v. Frederick, 551 U.S. 393 (2007).

34. Texas v. Johnson, 491 U.S. 397 (1989).

35. Spence v. Washington, 418 U.S. 405 (1974).

36. United States v. O'Brien, 391 U.S. 367 (1968).

37. Phoenix Elementary School District No. 1 v. Green, 943 P.2d 836 (Ariz. Ct. App. 1997).

38. 742 F.3d 1199 (9th Cir. 2014).

39. Naomi Sand, "Dress for Success," *The Pelican* (St. Paul's School, Concord, NH), April 28, 2011, http://spspelican.com/wp-content/uploads/2011/06/APRILFinalMaster3.pdf.

40. Ibid., 1.

41. Todd A. DeMitchell, Richard Fossey, and Casey Cobb, "Dress Codes in the Public Schools: Principals, Policies, and Precepts," *Journal of Law & Education* 29, no. 1 (2000): 31, 45.

Chapter One

School Uniforms and Dress Codes

From the Clothes Closet to the Courtroom

This is a tale without heroes and without villains.
—*Pyle v. South Hadley School Committee*, 1994[1]

SCHOOL UNIFORMS: DIFFERENT THAN DRESS CODES

Choosing what to wear to school in the morning would seem like an innocuous, rather benign decision for students to make as they start their day. But for some schoolchildren, the decision about what to wear to school is often a serious matter linked to their nascent development of self and place. For many others, the question revolves around what clean clothes are handy. "When left to decide what clothes to wear to school, students do not always make choices that adult agree with."[2]

The issue of what students wear to school often goes beyond the clothes closet to the courts. As schools struggle with problems of discipline and security, many have turned to the formulation of dress codes and most recently to mandatory school uniforms as a way to minimize controversy and potential disruptions around student clothing. For some school administrators, dress codes "have been justified as a means of creating a more disciplined learning environment."[3] However, other school leaders resist being put in the role of "fashion police." One elementary-school principal, when questioned about enforcing a school-uniform policy, responded, "My job is not to dress the public."[4]

Moreover, some school leaders have found that their efforts to more rigorously enforce student-dress regulations have not cut down on the controversy. Again and again, students and their parents have gone to court to oppose school rules about what students wear to school. Ironically, student dress codes and school-uniform policies, which had been implemented to cut down on the time school administrators were involved in clothing controversies, have triggered litigation in which educators and students are required to spend time in court rather than in the classroom.

In several lawsuits, the American Civil Liberties Union (ACLU) has joined students seeking to have a school dress code or school-uniform policy invalidated. For example, in Massachusetts, the principal of Lawrence High School sent out a letter to parents explaining the school's new mandatory school-uniform policy, stating, "We are optimistic that the new school uniform policy will help us to . . . create a more conducive learning environment within the school."[5] The Massachusetts ACLU responded in a news release, stating, "Apparently just the opposite is occurring. It is clear that many feel that personal dress is beyond the scope of the authority of the school. It is an issue of personal freedom. Such decisions should reside with students and their families. The ACLU concurs."[6]

The pushback by students to express themselves at school through their choice of clothing challenges two kinds of school regulations. First, students' demands to choose their attire often conflict with school dress codes, which define the clothes that students cannot wear to school. For example, schools often ban clothes that do not adequately cover the buttocks, breasts, and bellies, or clothes that advertise alcohol or drugs. In general, clothing that disrupts or is likely to disrupt the school is often the target of dress codes.[7] These kinds of student-clothing restrictions have seldom been associated with school reform. Rather, student dress codes are generally adopted to deal with student behavior or messages that can be distracting or disruptive in the school environment. Or as one federal court in Massachusetts put it, dress codes are a reasonable way to protect students from "an environment of unrelenting winks, snickering, and sexual proddings."[8]

Second, students and their parents have also challenged school policies that mandate what students must wear to school—in other words, school-uniform polices. A school district with a school-uniform policy may see its policy challenged on First Amendment grounds by students who insist they have a constitutional right not to wear a uniform while they are in school. Requiring students to wear uniforms to school, student plaintiffs assert, restricts their right to expressive conduct through their choice of clothing. While school uniforms often conjure visions of private,[9] often Catholic,[10] schools where girls wear plaid skirts and boys wear ties and jackets, most school-uniform policies in the public schools simply specify that students must wear clothing of a specific color combination, such as khaki and blue.

Without a doubt, school-uniform policies have become more popular over the years. President Clinton and former Secretary of Education Richard Riley expressed support for school uniforms as a way to reduce violence and maintain and enhance schools' learning environments as early as 1996.[11] Since that time, school uniforms have continued to be advanced as a positive strategy for reforming schools—touted as an effective means for improving student behavior, academics, and the overall school climate.

> There are interesting and important questions about the legal difference between dress codes (which limit the universe of clothing options) and mandatory uniform policies (which define the universe of clothing).
>
> Source: *Jacobs v. Clark County School District*, 526 F.3d 419, 444 (9th Cir. 2008) (Thomas, J., dissenting).

Although lawsuits against school dress codes and school-uniform policies often involve similar legal arguments, a school student-dress code is different from a school-uniform policy. School uniforms define what must be worn to school while dress codes define what must not be worn to school. Dress codes restrict clothing options for students while giving students a great deal of latitude about what they wear to school. On the other hand, mandatory school uniforms define students' clothing options within a narrow range.

Exemptions to Mandatory School Uniforms: Opting Out of Red and Khaki

A notable difference between dress codes and school uniforms is that schools with school-uniform policies often have regular opt-out days in which students are not required to wear uniforms to school. In contrast, schools with student dress codes never have days in which banned apparel can be worn to school. For example, schools do not designate days when students can wear sagging pants, immodest shirts and blouses, or T-shirts advertising alcohol.

The idea behind a school-uniform policy is that all students come to school dressed almost exactly alike (often with different dress requirements

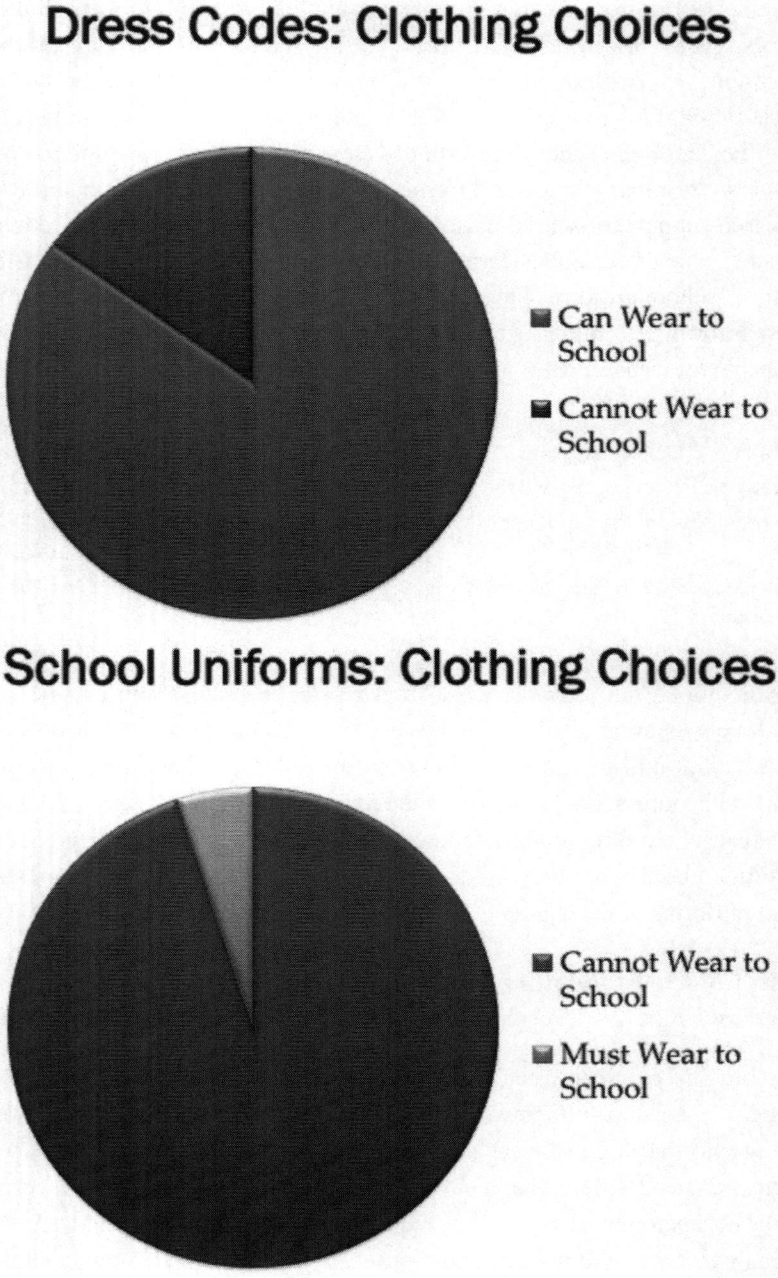
Dress Codes: Clothing Choices
Can Wear to School
Cannot Wear to School
School Uniforms: Clothing Choices
Cannot Wear to School
Must Wear to School

Figure 1.1.

for boys and girls). However, almost all schools with mandatory school-uniform policies allow some exceptions. For example, the US Department of Education *Manual on School Uniforms* listed two possible exceptions to the uniformity of the implementation of the policy. First, the *Manual* reads, "A uniform policy may not prohibit students from wearing or displaying expressive items—for example, a button that supports a political candidate—so long as such items do not independently contribute to disruption by substantially interfering with discipline or with the rights of others."[12] Second, the Department of Education's *Manual* states, "In most cases, school districts with mandatory policies allow students, normally with parental consent, to 'opt out' of the school uniform requirements."[13]

Thus, schools that adhere to the Department of Education's guidelines for school uniforms will permit students to wear expressive messages on their uniforms and allow some students to opt out of wearing school uniforms altogether. Thus, the question immediately comes to mind: at what point does the number of students who opt out of wearing uniforms or who wear individualized messages on their uniforms undermine benefits of the policy?[14] Where is the tipping point when the uniform look is no longer uniform?

Furthermore, for those schools that permit students to opt out of wearing the school uniform, what will be the basis for exempting particular students while requiring others to wear uniforms to school? Will exemptions be limited to families with religious objections, or will schools allow students to opt out of wearing school uniforms based on personal preferences? If families can exempt their children from wearing a uniform to school merely because they don't care for the way the uniform looks, there would seem to be little reason for requiring students to wear uniforms to school at all.

THE CONSTITUTION, THE PUBLIC SCHOOL, AND CLOTHING CHOICES

The Public School: Regulation and Restraint

Scholars and the courts have long recognized the public school as essential to the maintenance of an orderly and democratic society. Noted educational researchers David Tyack and Larry Cuban wrote, dialogue and debate about the goals of education are a "potent means of defining the present and shaping the future"; it is "one way that Americans make sense of their lives."[15] Questions about education go "to the heart of the kind of society we want to live in and the kind of society we want our children to live in."[16] Similarly, the US Supreme Court has regarded education as a matter of extreme importance. In *Plyler v. Doe*, the court wrote, "We have recognized the public schools as a most vital civic institution for preservation of a democratic system of government and as the primary vehicle for transmitting the values on which our society rests."[17]

The control of this vital institution rests with the elected local school board. They have broad discretion in the management of their schools. The authority to prescribe and control conduct in the schools is comprehensive.[18] However, that authority is not without limits. Actions taken in the public schools "must be exercised in a manner that comports with the transcendent imperatives of the First Amendment."[19] Thus, decisions made by school boards and carried out by professional educators must recognize and not conflict with the constitutional rights of students. All policies that control student attire are subject to this constitutional imperative.

Dress Codes and School Uniforms: Student Attire, but Different Approaches

While a school-uniform rule is different from a dress code, schools often implement either of these policies based on the desire to improve the learning environment and to cut down on disruptions that are related to student attire. However, regardless of whether a school district chooses to regulate student attire through a dress code or a uniform policy, any regulation of student dress can lead to litigation, with a student plaintiff claiming a violation of his or her constitutional rights. The constitutionality of dress codes as well as the wisdom of instituting school uniforms has been much debated in both the scholarly commentary and the courts, with arguments premised primarily on the First Amendment of the US Constitution.[20]

For example, the Somerset County Board of Education in Maryland required students at two elementary schools to wear khaki pants and dress shirts. The school board hoped the change of clothes would improve the education system. School Board Chairman Jack Willing stated that the new policy, slated to start in 2010–2011, would lead to less distractions in the classroom and less stress for parents, faculty, and students.[21] "Parents stress out about buying expensive clothes, students stress out about what they are going to wear that day in trying to keep up with their peers," said Willing. "The faculty have to worry about being fashion police and determining whether something is appropriate or not."[22]

I'm not sure if I think wearing a uniform every day benefited myself or the school community in any meaningful way. In fact, the policy created a lot of tension between students and the administration. One of our vice principals would stand in the lobby before school every morning checking to see if students' shirts were tucked in as they entered the building. Such rigid enforcement seemed ridiculous to most students (myself included), and definitely did not improve the climate of our school!

Kathryn O'Hearn
Graduate Student in Education
University of New Hampshire

Source: Quote used with the permission of Kathryn O'Hearn (December 9, 2014), on file with Todd DeMitchell.

Nevertheless, there is strong disagreement about the wisdom of implementing student-clothing policies—particularly school-uniform policies. The 2007–2008 *Public School Principal Questionnaire of the Schools and Staffing Survey*, administered by the National Center on Education Statistics, reported that of approximately 7,500 responding principals, 13.3 percent stated that they had implemented a school-uniform policy while 86.7 percent had not. This is compared to just over half (54.1 percent) of principals who had adopted a strict dress code (while 44.9 percent had not).[23]

An example of a school district reviewing whether to adopt a mandatory school-uniform policy occurred in 2009. The Long County Board of Education in Georgia rejected a recommendation from its superintendent to implement a school-uniform policy.[24] As is often the case in school dress-code disputes, the faculty and school administrators were in favor of implementing a school-uniform policy, but the parents were not. On the other hand, the Bradford County School Board in Florida voted to continue its school-uniform policy at the middle school in spite of a parent survey that was nearly two to one against the policy.[25]

School-uniform policy debates focus on the effect of mandatory uniforms on student behavior and outcomes. These debates differ somewhat from policy discussions about dress codes, which are often, but not exclusively, developed in response to problems associated with specific types of attire. For example, a school issued a ban on middle school students wearing bracelets with the following inscription, "I ♥ Boobies! (KEEP A BREAST)."[26] The ban was drafted specifically to address a concern about the propriety of wearing the wrist bands even though the message about breast cancer was consistent with the school's message. The ban was not instituted to solve a more generalized concern. Similarly, in *Boroff v. Van Wert City Board of Education*, school authorities invoked the dress code to prohibit a student from wearing a Marilyn Manson T-shirt to school.[27] The T-shirt depicted a three-faced Jesus with the inscription "See No Truth Hear No Truth Speak No Truth."

However, an example of how school uniforms may have a different genesis is illustrated by the Marion Community Schools' adoption of a school-uniform policy for McCulloch Middle School in Fort Wayne, Indiana starting in the fall of 2008.[28] The policy was adopted "to address student behavior and academic issues at the school."[29] In the three school years prior to the adoption, the school had over three thousand disciplinary referrals and had not made Adequate Yearly Progress under the state school accountability guidelines in five years.[30]

The school-uniform policy was not aimed at the inappropriate dress of its students. Rather, the policy was adopted to bring about changes in students' educational environment and to improve their academic performance by mandating the wearing of specific clothes. The school board and its educators believed the uniform policy would make a positive difference by helping to improve student performance and academic achievement, instilling discipline, and preparing students to be productive citizens by teaching them how to "dress for success."[31]

Proponents of school uniforms align policy with desired educational outcomes and reform whereas dress-code proponents develop their policies in response to a problem associated with student dress. For example, former President Clinton and former Secretary of Education Richard Riley supported the role of uniforms in reducing violence and establishing an environment for students and adults that is conducive to learning.[32] School uniforms have been advanced as a positive strategy to reform schools in terms of behavior, academics, and school climate.

THE POLITICAL CHALLENGE OF IMPLEMENTING MANDATORY SCHOOL UNIFORMS

Does a student's morning ritual of searching through the closet to find clean clothes to wear to school implicate the US Constitution? Does the selection of pants (yoga pants, shorts, jeans, etc.) and tops (with written statements, or crop tops, etc.) deserve the protection of the First Amendment? The answer to these questions has been mixed depending on the clothes selected and the dress code of the school. While educators are on the front line in responding to these questions, it is often the courts that provide the final answer. And, unfortunately, the answer does not always provide a clear path for educators to follow, because the courts have not ruled consistently.

In short, the debate about school policies that restrict students' clothing choices involve two dimensions. First, do schools have the authority to regulate their students' clothing choices without violating their right to free expression under the First Amendment? Second, what constitutes good education policy: is it good public policy for school authorities to tell students what they can and cannot wear to school, regardless of whether they have the legal authority to do so?

Thus, adopting a school-uniform policy is not a simple matter. Forces of opposition often coalesce in response to proposed school-uniform policies along both dimensions. We will review the response to proposed school uniforms from New Hampshire. It provides a window into how parents and students push against policies that they perceive as restricting their individual rights and prerogatives.

> "[B]ecause nobody likes uniforms. [I] would look like an eighty-five-year-old woman."
>
> —Ocean Valdez, responding to an online petition against the proposed Pinkerton Academy school uniform policy
>
> Source: Change.org, *Pinkerton Academy "Unified Dress Code" (Uniforms): Stop the Uniform Proposal*, 2013, available at https://www.change.org/petitions/pinkerton-academy-unified-dress-code-uniforms-stop-the-uniform-proposal.

An online petition against Pinkerton Academy's proposed "Unified Dress Code" gathered 285 signatures against the proposed code.[33] The new school-attire policy, which essentially mandated school uniforms,[34] was expected to replace the existing dress code.[35] The petition, initiated by Savana Melanson, stated, "[A school uniform] takes away individuality. Also it will not change the study habits of students. Too much money for each child, parents do not have that type of money especially in this economy. We have the right to freedom of expression and would like to keep it that way."[36] The responses supporting the petition to stop the proposed school-uniform policy capture much of the broader debate across the nation about adopting mandatory school uniform policies.

For example, petitioners wrote:

- "I do not want my freedom of expression taken away." Alinah Domings
- "Its [sic] my right to wake up in the morning and have my own unique individuality." Jade Catizone
- "The way I dress, act, and speak are how I express my induvality [sic]. At school, the way I act and speak is already limited and surpressed [sic], but I can tolerate that! Trying to crush it further with a school uniform?!
- "Absolutely not!" Tatiana McNeil[37]

The petitioners, many of them students, but some parents as well, based their arguments against school uniforms on three pillars—freedom of speech/expression, the cost of the uniforms,[38] and the belief that the school uniforms will not solve issues (behavior/student achievement) at the school.[39] The academy's final decision was to maintain the current "business casual" dress code rather than implement the proposed Unified Dress Code.[40]

School districts across the nation struggle with the same policy considerations that the New Hampshire district confronted.[41] There is no clear decision about whether school uniforms are good for public education, let alone whether a school-uniform policy is the right policy decision for a specific school.

"The Mark of the Beast"

An interesting application of a school-uniform policy is found in a 2013 case out of Texas. The facts of this case are different from the cases explored in chapter 4, and is placed here as background.

The Northside Independent School District required students to carry a nametag with their photo and school campus listed. Employees also wore similar badges and all visitors were required to wear the badges as well. In addition, the school had digital cameras installed throughout the campus to help provide a safe and secure school environment. The nametag, similar to a school uniform, was meant to easily identify intruders.

A pilot project was started to further increase safety and security. Smart ID badges were introduced at two schools: a high school and a middle school. Each Smart ID badge, in addition to displaying the student's photograph, name, and campus, had an implanted radio frequency identification (RFID) chip. Through the use of sensors planted throughout the school, school authorities could ascertain the whereabouts of all students. The RFID badges were "expected to improve safety" by allowing school staff to know the location of a student who might be missing or unaccounted for during a fire drill or emergency evacuation.

A. H., a fifteen-year-old sophomore, acting through her parents, objected to the RFID badges. Her parents claimed, "if we compromise our faith and religious freedom to allow you to track my daughter while she is at school it will condemn us to hell."[42] In the parents' view, an RFID badge was "the mark of the beast."[43] The superintendent responded that A. H. would not have to wear a badge with the RFID chip in it but she would have to wear the new badge as she had done before with the old badge. The parents rejected the compromise, stating that wearing the badge would require their daughter to "fall in line like the rest of them," and force her to sell out by compromising her faith and disobeying "our Lord and Savior."[44] They brought suit seeking a preliminary injunction to stop the school from enforcing its relaxed policy that would require her to wear the designated school badge without the RFID chip.

The federal district court treated the badge requirement as if it were a school-uniform policy that applied to all students. The court noted that other courts had upheld school-uniform policies that had been adopted for such purposes as promoting respect for authority or boosting school spirit. Surely, the court reasoned, "the safety and security of the students and educators is a more compelling interest than promoting school spirit, decorum, respect for authority and decreasing socioeconomic tension." Thus, the court concluded, "[i]f mandatory school uniform policies pass constitutional muster, a mandatory student ID requirement surely passes constitutional muster."[45]

Court decisions involving student dress codes are considerably less consistent rulings on school-uniform policies. In fact, dress-code litigation tends to look more like potpourri than a unified, articulated body of case law. As we noted fifteen years ago, "Unanimity on the issue of the constitutionality of dress codes had not been achieved, leaving a large degree of uncertainty in the courts."[46] And this state of affairs has not changed. Thus far, students have been more successful in challenging student dress codes than mandatory school-uniform policies. The paradox is that students have some success contesting the lesser restrictions of a dress code and almost no success in contesting the more restrictive mandatory school-uniform policies, and this has been true regardless of the constitutional theory under which students litigate.

Dress codes prohibit wearing specific styles or types of clothing, leaving a large spectrum of options for student choice of wearing apparel, while school-uniform policies place strict mandates on what students can wear, often leaving them no clothing choice except the decision to wear blue rather than khaki. Both restrict what students wear to school. But both types of policies place the interests of the school above the rights of students to make their own clothing choices.

> If every time a citizen was outraged by the workings of a rather unimaginative bureaucracy he claimed a harm of constitutional dimensions, the courts would not just be crowded—they would be paralyzed.
>
> Source: *Swany v. San Ramon Valley Unified School District,* 720 F. Supp. 764, 783 (N.D. Calif. 1989).

The Supreme Court has recognized that schools have a "compelling interest in having an undisrupted school session conducive to the students' learning."[47] Where to place the fulcrum to balance the competing interests is the policy challenge. School districts are not required to adopt either a dress code or a mandatory school uniform, but states often allow such a choice. The policy choice is a discretionary act on the part of the elected school board.[48] That choice often conflicts with the wishes and desires of students and their parents. Case analysis and a review of the research can assist board members as they make their decisions. We will turn to these next.

NOTES

1. Pyle By and Through Pyle v. South Hadley School Committee, 861 F. Supp. 157, 173 (D.Mass. 1994).
2. Linda Lumsden and Gabriel Miller, "Dress Codes and Uniforms," *Research Roundup* (2002): 1. Available at www.naesp.org/misc/rrsum02.htm.

3. Rob Killen, "The Achilles' Heel of Dress Codes: The Definition of Proper Attire in Public Schools," *Tulsa Law Journal* 36 (2000): 461.

4. Matthew Goldstein, "Parents to Sort Out School Wardrobe," *Boston Sunday Globe*, April 20, 2003.

5. American Civil Liberties Union of Massachusetts, "All This in the Name of Order," News Release, April 24, 2001, available athttp://www.aol.com./mcluf/lawr.

6. Ibid.

7. However, Tinker v. Des Moines Independent Community School District, 393 U.S. 503, 514 (1969) essentially found that student, passive, nondisruptive political speech (wearing a black armband in protest of the War in Vietnam) during school hours is protected speech.

8. Pyle By and Through Pyle v. South Hadley School Committee, 861 F. Supp 157, 170 (D.Mass. 1994).

9. Michael Firmin, Suzanne Smith, and Lynsey Perry, *School Uniforms: A Qualitative Analysis of Aims and Accomplishments at Two Schools* (Cedar University). A parent in a study of school uniforms at two Christian schools stated, "When they are out in our society, they're representing . . . [the school] . . . and we hope that with them being in those uniforms it would be a reminder to them that they are from a Christian school and they are to put forth a Godly appearance as a witness." Available at http://www.albany.edu/eqre/papers/21EQRE.doc.

10. See Susan McBrayer, "The School Uniform Movement and What It Tells Us about American Education: A Symbolic Crusade," *Catholic Education* (September 2007). "The plaid uniform has been culturally synonymous with Catholic schools. Today, however, uniforms have become less formal, replacing dress shirts for polo shirts emblazoned with the school name or mascot. Sweaters and blazers have given way to sweatshirts in many Catholic schools. Administrators and teachers may have initiated this change in keeping with the more secular phenomenon of 'business casual.' Furthermore, rising tuition, declining enrollment, and a change in demographics may have also contributed to new trends in the Catholic school uniform." http://findarticles.com/p/articles/mi_6936/is_1_11/ai_n28543541/pg_2/?tag=content ;col1.

11. See William Jefferson Clinton, "Remarks by the President on School Uniform Program," Jackie Robinson Academy, Long Beach, California, February 24, 1996, http://www.ed.gov/pressreleases/02-1996/whpr28 and US Department of Education, *Manual on School Uniforms* (1996), http://www.ed.gov/updates/uniforms.

12. *Manual on School Uniforms*, available at http://www.ed.gov/updates/uniforms.html.

13. Ibid.

14. For an example of the use of an opt-out policy by a group of parents and community members who are opposed to a school-uniform policy, see *Stop School Uniforms in Osceola County*, http://www.petitiononline.com/sou1/petition.html. A petition with 2,144 signatures was signed. The petition stated in pertinent part regarding the use of an opt-out provision:

> We require that the School Board provide empirical evidence of its own that their uniform policy will significantly improve the safety of our children without impacting their academic success. Absent such evidence, if the School Board wishes to adopt a uniform policy, we require that any such policy be voluntary and contain an opt-out clause that affords constitutional protection to those who wish to assert it. The opt-out process must be simple and undeniable; American citizens should not be made to meet onerous bureaucratic requirements to prove or substantiate their beliefs or to meet arbitrary time constraints to opt-out.

15. David Tyack and Larry Cuban, *Tinkering Toward Utopia: A Century of Public School Reform* (Cambridge, MA: Harvard University Press, 1997), 42.

16. Lawrence A. Cremin, *Public Education* (New York: Basic Books, 1976), 75.

17. Plyler v. Doe, 457 U.S. 202, 221 (1982).

18. Board of Education, Island Trees Union Free School District No. 26 v. Pico, 457 U.S. 853, 863–64 (1982).

19. Ibid., 864.

20. Todd A. DeMitchell and Mark A. Paige, "School Uniforms in the Public Schools: Symbol or Substance? A Law & Policy Analysis," *Education Law Reporter* 250 (2010): 847.

21. Policy Guidelines for Policy #600-12 state that the mandatory school uniform must be worn daily except for designated casual days in the elementary schools and in the intermediate school. The high school is exempt from the regulation. It is interesting to note that the end of the administrative guideline states, "These guidelines in no way is [sic] intended to prevent a student from attending school." School Uniform Information Somerset County Schools, available at http://www.somerset.k12.md.us/BOE/SchoolBoard/BoardPolicies/Policies/600-12ap.pdf.

22. Brie Jackson, "Two Somerset County Schools to Start Wearing Uniforms," *WBOC 16, WBOC News*, May 29, 2009, http://www.wboc.com/Global/story.asp?S=10439682&nav=MXEF.

23. See National Center for Education Statistics, Schools and Staffing Survey, http://nces.ed.gov/surveys/sass/question0708.asp.

24. Mike Riddle, "Long BoE Nixes Student Uniforms," *Coastal Courier*, May 29, 2009, http://www.coastalcourier.com/news/article/14193/.

25. Mark J. Crawford, "Board Ignores Survey to Support Uniforms," *Bradford County Telegraph*, May 28, 2009, http://www.zwire.com/site/news.cfm?newsid=20321977&BRD=2150&PAG=461&dept_id=377017&rfi=6 (accessed May 30, 2009). A review of the Student Code of Conduct on August 17, 2011 showed that the school uniform for the Bradford Middle School was still in place as of August 2011 (Superintendent's Letter to Parents) and was the only school with a mandatory school uniform policy. http://www.mybradford.us/files/_TJCFl_/9acd9ad45c162b5a3745a49013852ec4/11-12_Student_Code_of_conduct_-_Bd._App_-_FINAL.pdf.

26. B.H. v. Easton Area School District, 725 F.3d 293 (3d Cir. 2013).

27. Boroff v. Van Wert City Board of Education, 240 F.3d 465 (6th Cir. 2000).

28. McCulloch Junior High School Student Handbook 33–42 (2011–2012). Available at http://www.marion.k12.in.us/mcculloch.cfm?subpage=816.

29. Derry v. Marion Community Schools, 790 F. Supp. 2d 839, 845 (N.D. Ind. 2008).

30. Ibid.

31. Ibid., 846.

32. See William Jefferson Clinton, "Remarks by the President on School Uniform Program," Jackie Robinson Academy, Long Beach, California, February 24, 1996, http://www.ed.gov/pressreleases/02-1996/whpr28; US Department of Education, *Manual on School Uniforms* (1996), available at http://www.ed.gov/updates/uniforms.

33. Change.org, *Pinkerton Academy "Unified dress code" (uniforms): Stop the uniform proposal* (2013), available at https://www.change.org/petitions/pinkerton-academy-unified-dress-code-uniforms-stop-the-uniform-proposal. As of June 1, 2014, the 715 needed number of supporters for the petition was not met.

34. The school administrators at Pinkerton Academy did not characterize the unified dress code as a school uniform. Hunter McGee, "Derry's Pinkerton Academy Looks at Narrowing

Dress Code," *New Hampshire Union Leader*, September 22, 2013, http://www.unionleader.com/article/20130923/NEWS04/130929754.

35. For a copy of the dress code, see Pinkerton Academy 2013–2014 Student Planner, at 4, available at http://www.pinkertonacademy.net/resources/documents/Student%20Planner%202013-14.pdf.

36. Change.org, note 33.

37. Ibid.

38. See this response from Solon Rawson: "One major problem is that the cost is simply unfeasible [not] for just the impoverished students and families, but for the middle class who is still hard-hit by the recession. It is exponentially more viable for families to buy their clothing second-hand, and making everyone wear the same thing would amplify the differences between 'new' clothing and 'used' clothing." Ibid.

39. See Lauren Finney, "I believe a healthy wholesome lunch would actually increase productivity exponentially more than a unified dress code, we need more broccoli and less mechanically separated chicken"; Michael Szekely, "I neither want uniforms, nor do I think it will solve any problems"; Carla Duarte, "Changing my clothes into something that makes me feel self-conscious and uncomfortable is not going to turn me into a better student." Ibid.

40. Glenn Ahrens, Dean of Students, Pinkerton Academy, letter to families of students of Pinkerton Academy, April 4, 2014, available at http://www.pinkertonacademy.net/announcements/April%204.pdf.

41. For example, parents in Texas have organized against school uniforms by establishing websites such as "Mandatory School Uniforms—Not!" March 8, 2001. Available at http://mandatoryschooluniform.org/. See also *supra* note 14 for a Florida website.

42. A.H. v. Northside Independent School District, 916 F. Supp. 2d 757, 763 (W.D. Tex. 2013).

43. Ibid. See Revelation 13:16–17 for the full scripture.

44. Ibid., 764.

45. Ibid., 772.

46. Todd A. DeMitchell, Richard Fossey, and Casey Cobb, "Dress Codes in the Public Schools: Principals, Policies, and Precepts," *Journal of Law & Education* 29, no. 1 (2000): 46.

47. Grayned v. City of Rockford, 408 U.S. 104, 119 (1972).

48. See Pickup v. Brown, 728 F.3d 1042, 1066 (9th Cir. 2013), writing, "Parents have a constitutionally protected right to make decisions regarding the care, custody, and control of their children, but that right is 'not without limitations.' States may require school attendance and mandatory school uniforms, and they may impose curfew laws applicable only to minors."

Chapter Two

Student Free Speech and Clothing Choices

It is perhaps, the most basic of questions in First Amendment jurisprudence: what constitutes speech?[1]

WHAT IS FREE SPEECH?

The issue of student speech is important for school administrators because as Nelda Cambron-McCabe stated, "School officials confront students' speech rights on a daily basis in public schools."[2] Attorneys Brandt, Skinner, and Kelley characterize schools as "incubators of constitutional litigation."[3] Gaining an understanding of students' First Amendment rights while they are in school is imperative for understanding the legal issues surrounding student dress codes and school uniforms. This legal controversy stems from the assertion that "dress can qualify as conduct that meets the standard of symbolic speech, which is entitled to First Amendment protection."[4] It is noteworthy that no student dress-code case has been argued before the US Supreme Court. However, the High Court has provided some guidance with respect to the parameters of student freedom of expression that occurs at school, which we will explore below.

The First Amendment to the United States Constitution states, in pertinent part, that "Congress shall make no law . . . abridging the freedom of speech or of the press."[5] The importance of free speech to the concept of what it means to be an American cannot be overstated. The right to free speech builds a foundation for the relationship between citizens and their government. It is a right that neither the Magna Carta of 1215 nor the English Bill of Rights of 1689 protected for citizens. (However, the English Bill of Rights protected free speech for members of Parliament.) The right to free speech is characterized as the touchstone, the wellspring of individual liberty. Free speech is a hearty, robust right, not a mere shadow of a right that hues to bland, uneventful speech.[6]

For example, Justice Cardozo described freedom of speech as "the matrix, the indispensable condition of nearly every other form of freedom."[7] Over three-quarters of a century ago, the Supreme Court wrote, "Freedom of speech and freedom of press, which are protected by the First Amendment from infringement by Congress, are among the fundamental personal rights and liberties, which are protected by the Fourteenth Amendment from invasion by state action."[8] In 1995, the Supreme Court opined that the purpose of the Bill of Rights generally and the First Amendment particularly, "is to protect unpopular individuals from retaliation and their ideas from suppression at the hand of an intolerant society."[9]

Professor Alexander Meiklejohn echoes these sentiments from the Supreme Court about the importance of free speech to the individual but adds the dimension he deems necessary for self-government. He writes, "The unabridged freedom of public discussion is the rock on which our government stands."[10] Similarly, the Court wrote that free speech serves society by allowing the "uninhibited, robust, and wide-open debates about matters of public importance that secures an informed citizenry."[11]

Consequently, the right to free speech in our society is extensive and robust.[12] Supporting this view, Justice Holmes observed, "it is . . . not free thought for those who agree with us, but freedom for thought we hate."[13] Another example of the breadth and depth of the First Amendment right to free speech is found in a Supreme Court case involving race-baiting speech. The High Court wrote "[a] function of free speech under our system of government is to invite dispute. It may indeed best serve its high purpose when it induces a condition of unrest, creates dissatisfaction with conditions as they are, or even stirs people to anger. Speech is often provocative and challenging."[14] Law Professor Cass Sunstein offers an interesting view of the limitations of government to regulate speech, especially political speech. He wrote that "government cannot insult the moral autonomy of its citizens by stopping them from hearing what other people say—especially if the reason that government acts is its fear that citizens will be influenced or persuaded by what is said."[15]

While the terms are often used interchangeably, the concept of civil liberties and the concept of civil rights are different, with each providing distinct protections. Free speech is considered a civil liberty as opposed to a civil right. Civil liberties are protections against government actions. Most often civil liberties concern the freedoms guaranteed in the Bill of Rights, which places explicit prohibitions on the power of government. Civil liberties often restrict government action, whereas a civil right requires government to take positive action to protect an individual from unequal treatment.

One of Americans' most important civil rights is grounded in the Equal Protection Clause of the Fourteenth Amendment, which guarantees that all Americans are entitled to equal protection under the law. Often, in the pursuit of civil rights, the government balances the will of majority with the rights of minorities. The former is a person's liberty from actions of government, "which leave the individual free to think and sometimes to act as he or she chooses without interference from government."[16] The latter, civil rights, is a right of the individual protected by the affirmative actions of government.

THE LIMITS OF FREE SPEECH

The First Amendment does not protect such vague and attenuated notions of expression—namely, self-expression through any and all clothing that a 12-year-old may wish to wear on a given day.

Source: *Blau v. Fort Thomas Public School District*, 401 F.3d 381,389 (6th Cir. 2005).

However, as robust as the right of free speech is under our Constitution, it is not without limits. Indeed, the Supreme Court, writing nearly one hundred years ago, asserted that the right of free speech, while "sacred and vital," "is not absolute, it is subject to restriction and limitation."[17]

Content of the Speech

"If there is a bedrock principle underlying the First Amendment it is that the government may not prohibit the expression of an idea simply because society finds the idea itself offensive or disagreeable."[18] Thus, government restrictions on speech that are based on the content of the speech face a presumption of invalidity when reviewed by the courts. An assessment of whether a regulation is content-related or content-neutral depends on "whether the government has adopted a regulation of speech because of disagreement with the message it conveys."[19]

Professor Erwin Chermerinsky writes, "All speech, regardless of its content, must be treated the same by government. To allow the government to target particular views or subjects permits the government to greatly distort the marketplace of ideas."[20] Essentially, given the power of government over individuals, it cannot overpower the message that it disagrees with and trumpet the message that it prefers; otherwise, "government may effectively drive out certain ideas or viewpoints form the marketplace."[21] Government regulations must be neutral regarding the content of the message or they must meet the highest burden of strict-scrutiny analysis in order for the regulation to pass constitutional muster.

An example of government suppressing speech through a content-related regulation is found in *R.A.V. v. St. Paul*, in which the St. Paul Bias-Motivated Crime Ordinance was struck down.[22] The Supreme Court held that a bias-motivated crime ordinance violated the First Amendment because it punished fighting words motivated by race, color, creed, religion, or gender hostility, but not those motivated by other reasons. The ordinance punished certain viewpoints but not others, and the government may not regulate speech "based on hostility—or favoritism—towards the underlying message expressed."[23] The ordinance was used to prosecute someone for burning a cross on the lawn of an African American family. While the Supreme Court, in a somewhat fractured opinion, found the act to be reprehensible, it also found that the ordinance suppressed speech.

Governmental agencies that promulgate content-related regulations that suppress speech come to the courts with a heavy burden of proving constitutionality, while content-neutral regulations may shoulder a lighter load. If a dress code is considered content-neutral—in other words, it is not aimed at suppressing specific speech—it has a greater chance of success. An example of a content-neutral regulation is the dress code passed in Waxahachie Independent School District, which banned school-uniform shirts that displayed any printed message other than messages pertaining to school spirit that were approved by the school principal. In essence, virtually all shirt-based speech was prohibited; thus the regulation did not single out a particular message to suppress. The Fifth Circuit Court of Appeals, in a lawsuit challenging the constitutionality of the dress code, asserted, "[t]he District was in no way attempting to suppress any student's expression through its dress code—a critical fact based on earlier student speech cases—so the dress code is content-neutral."[24]

> [N]o matter how well-intentioned the stated objective, once schools get into the business of actively promoting one political or religious viewpoint over another, there is no end to the mischief that can be done in the name of good intentions.
>
> Source: *Hansen v. Ann Arbor Public Schools*, 293 F. Supp. 2d 780, 803 (E.D. Mich. 2003).

In *Linmark Associates, Inc. v. Town of Willingboro* (1977), the Supreme Court noted that laws regulating the time, place, and manner of speech are different than those regulations that prohibit speech.[25] Time, place, and manner restrictions that do not treat speech differently based on the content of the speech and leave open ample alternative means of expression typically do not violate free-speech rights. For example, school regulations that designate the place and times in which students can distribute literature need to be reasonable and nondiscriminatory. The regulations must apply uniformly to all speech (content neutral); and for a school, the regulations must be related to the function of the school.[26]

Unprotected Speech

Free speech is indeed a critical right that is protected in our society. It is a right that is often used as the example of what it means to be an American and to be free. However, the right to free speech is not absolute. The courts, when reviewing free speech challenges, must parse the difference between the regulation of speech and the suppression of speech. They "are not the same, either in purpose or result."[27] Regulation is permissible when government is not trying to suppress the content of ideas, except in very specific circumstances such as fighting words,[28] incitement to riot producing imminent lawless action,[29] defamation,[30] child pornography,[31] obscenity,[32] and true threats.[33]

Moreover, the Supreme Court has made clear that the free-speech rights of students while at school are not as full-bodied as the free-speech rights of adults. "Students are free to express themselves in many ways outside the schoolhouse gate, but inside the schoolhouse gate it is another matter."[34] Even though students do not shed their constitutional right to free speech at the schoolhouse gate,[35] school officials have the authority to put some restrictions on student speech, as outlined in four Supreme Court decisions, which we will discuss in the next section.

STUDENT FREE-SPEECH CASES: THE SUPREME COURT DECIDES

In a T-shirt case in Massachusetts, a federal court judge opined, "At least in high school, a political message does not justify a vulgar medium."

Source: *Pyle By and Through Pyle v. South Hadley School Committee*, 861 F. Supp. 157, 169 (D.Mass. 1994).

Law Professor Robert C. Post asserted that, historically, there was widespread judicial deference to the judgment of school officials.[36] Until the middle of the twentieth century, the courts imposed little or no obligation on the public schools to respect the constitutional rights of their students. But in *Shelton v. Tucker*, decided in 1967, the Supreme Court made clear that students enjoyed constitutional rights in the school environment. "The vigilant protection of constitutional freedoms is nowhere more vital than in the community of American schools," the Court stated. [37]

For example, in *New Jersey v. T.L.O.*, decided in 1985, the Supreme Court ruled that students have a constitutional right to privacy under the Fourth Amendment, which they do not give up when they come onto school grounds; and school officials cannot disregard that right simply because they desire to search a student's person or possessions.[38] Students also have a constitutional right to due process before being suspended or expelled from school, which the Supreme Court recognized in 1975.[39] However, students have not been successful in asserting that paddling (corporal punishment) rises to the level of a constitutional violation under the Eighth Amendment's prohibition against cruel and unusual punishment.[40]

Students also have a constitutional right to free speech, but that right is not unfettered. "The very nature of public education requires limitations on one's personal liberty in order for learning process to proceed."[41] Thus, a student's right to free speech must be balanced against the need of the state to provide an efficient system of public education. Public schools inculcate fundamental values necessary to the maintenance of a democratic society.

These fundamental values include "habits and manners of civility."[42] Although toleration of divergent views and unpopular views is important to civility, sensibility to others, including fellow students, is also important. As Chief Justice Burger observed, "The undoubted freedom to advocate unpopular and controversial views in schools and classrooms must be balanced against the society's countervailing interest in teaching students the boundaries of socially appropriate behavior."[43]

Symbolic Protest: *Tinker v. Des Moines Independent Community School District*

Mary Beth Tinker wrote, "In 1965, I was the 13-year-old who, along with a group of students including my brother John and our friend Chris Eckhardt, was suspended for wearing black armbands to a Des Moines, Iowa school to mourn the dead in Vietnam. For that, we faced harassment and even death threats."

Source: Mary Beth Tinker, "Standing Up for the Rights of Students to Free Expression," *ACLU Blog of Rights*, May 24, 2013, available at https://www.aclu.org/blog/free-speech/standing-rights-students-free-expression.

It has been over forty years since the Supreme Court extended the protection of the First Amendment to students inside the schoolhouse gate.[44] In 1965, John and Mary Beth Tinker and Chris Eckhart were suspended by Des Moines School officials for wearing black armbands to school in protest of the Vietnam War. The school administration took this action based on a hastily developed policy that had been implemented specifically in response to the students' planned protest.

The three students brought suit in federal court arguing that the First Amendment gave them the right to express themselves in this quiet and dignified way, but a federal district court dismissed their complaint. On appeal, the Eighth Circuit Court of Appeals heard the case *en banc*, but the court was equally divided and thus affirmed the trial court's dismissal of the students' constitutional claims. The two fifteen- and sixteen-year-olds and thirteen-year-old Mary Beth Tinker then proceeded to the US Supreme Court to press their case that they had a constitutional right to quietly and passively wear a two-inch-wide black armband in protest of the war in Vietnam.

In *Tinker v. Des Moines Independent Community School District*, the Supreme Court reversed the lower courts' decisions and recognized the Tinker children's right to wear black armbands to school in protest of the Vietnam War. Students in school as well as out of school "are 'persons' under the Constitution," the court wrote. "They are possessed of fundamental rights that the state must respect, just as they themselves must respect their obligations to the State,"[45] although school officials possess "the comprehensive authority . . . to prescribe and control conduct in the schools."[46] Martha McCarthy, noted school-law professor, described *Tinker* as the Magna Carta for student free-speech rights.[47]

However, the Court found limits to the control that can be exerted over public-school students, asserting:

> In our system, state-operated schools may not be enclaves of totalitarianism. School officials do not possess absolute authority over their students. . . . In our system, students may not be regarded as closed-circuit recipients of only that which the State chooses to communicate. They may not be confined to the expression of those sentiments that are officially approved.[48]

The Supreme Court found that school authorities could not justify the prohibition of student expression at school unless the conduct would "materially and substantially interfere with the requirements of appropriate discipline in the operation of the school"[49] or "collid[es] with the rights of others."[50] The court asserted that "undifferentiated fear or apprehension of disturbance" cannot trump this "hazardous freedom" and replace it with rigid regimentation.[51]

Using this line of reasoning, a restriction on student clothing that arguably had some symbolic or explicit expression must be supported by a finding that the clothing "materially disrupts classwork or involves substantial disorder."[52] Second, student speech may be prohibited when it involves a "collision with the rights of other students to be secure and to be let alone."[53] This standard raised the question of whether all clothing choices are protected as long as they do not create a material and substantial disruption.

Courts have cited *Tinker* many times over the years in cases involving the free-expression rights of public-school students in their choice of clothing and appearance. Unfortunately, few of these cases involved issues as noble as the one the Tinkers brought forward. In fact, the High Court in *Tinker* expressly differentiated protected speech from dress codes. The Supreme Court wrote: "The problem posed by the present case does not relate to the regulation of the length of skirts or the type of clothing. Our problem involves direct, primary First Amendment rights akin to 'pure speech.'"[54] Nevertheless, in spite of the fact that the Supreme Court differentiated between pure speech and clothing issues, courts have cited *Tinker* for the proposition that a student's choice of style of clothing may carry the protection of the US Constitution.

For example, the Fourth Circuit of Appeals, applying *Tinker*, supported a student wearing a T-shirt with the three black silhouettes holding rifles with "NRA" stamped over the silhouettes. The court found that the T-shirts were not disruptive.[55] Similarly, cases involving wearing the Confederate flag often use the *Tinker* test to resolve the issue.[56]

Lewd, Vulgar, and Offensive Speech: *Bethel School District v. Fraser*

Since the *Tinker* decision first acknowledged the free-speech rights of students in the school environment, three more Supreme Court decisions "[have]expanded the kinds of speech schools can regulate."[57] Some consider *Tinker* as the "high water mark" for student free expression and the subsequent Supreme Court decisions as a retrenchment.[58]

Seventeen years after *Tinker*, the Supreme Court decided a case that would dramatically impact students' rights of expression at school. In *Bethel School District No. 403 v. Fraser*,[59] the Supreme Court ruled that school officials could sanction a high-school student for using lewd, vulgar, or offensive sexual metaphors during a political speech at a school assembly. Mathew Fraser gave a nomination speech filled with graphic language laden with explicit sexual language but no profanities. Some students in the school assembly "hooted and yelled" and made sexual gestures in response to his speech, while other students sat bewildered and embarrassed.

After a due process hearing with the assistant principal, Fraser received a three-day suspension for using obscene language in violation of the school's discipline code, and his name was removed from the candidate graduation speaker list.[60] Fraser contested the discipline in federal district court alleging a violation of First Amendment right to free speech.

The District Court held for Fraser, asserting that the school's disruptive conduct rule was vague and overbroad. It awarded Fraser $278 in damages and $12,750 in litigation costs and attorney's fees. The school district appealed but lost before the Ninth Circuit Court of Appeals. The Circuit Court found that Fraser's speech was "indistinguishable" from Tinker's armband.[61] The school district appealed.

The Supreme Court accepted certiorari and reversed the lower courts' decisions finding for the defendant school district instead. In declaring that the school district had the authority to sanction Fraser for his vulgar speech, the Supreme Court chose not to apply the *Tinker* standard of material and substantial disruption, and instead fashioned a new analysis and test. The Supreme Court stated emphatically that the public schools have the duty to "inculcate the habits and manners of civility."[62] This fundamental value of civility, the court pointed out, must take into account the "sensibilities of others."[63]

As one commentator opined, "This statement, coupled with *Tinker's* collision with the rights of others, tends to support dress codes aimed at supporting a civil school environment."[64] As the Supreme Court pointed out in *Fraser*, our nation's leaders have rules against offensive expression in our nation's legislative halls, where vigorous political debate often occurs. Could the Supreme Court expect no less degree of civility in our schools? Or as the Supreme Court put it, "Can it be that what is proscribed in the halls of Congress is beyond the reach of school officials to regulate?"[65]

The Supreme Court, in *Fraser*, held that "[t]he determination of what manner of speech in the classroom or in a school assembly is inappropriate properly rests with the school board."[66] Thus, the Court upheld a school district's right to prohibit speech that is lewd, vulgar, or laced with sexual innuendo. "Surely it is a highly appropriate function of public education to prohibit vulgar and offensive terms in public discourse."[67]

Furthermore, the court affirmed that the constitutional rights of students in public schools are not automatically coextensive with the rights of adults in other settings. While adults have wide freedom in matters of public discourse, it does not follow that the same latitude must be permitted to children in P–12 public school. As cogently expressed by Judge Newman and quoted by the Supreme Court, "the First Amendment gives a high school student the classroom right to wear Tinker's armband, but not Cohen's jacket."[68]

The Supreme Court's rationale in the *Fraser* decision was applied by the Sixth Circuit Court of Appeals, which held that a Marilyn Manson T-shirt of a three-headed Jesus with the wording "See No Truth, Hear No Truth, Speak No Truth" was vulgar, offensive, and contrary to the mission of the school.[69] Because the T-shirt was vulgar, the Sixth Circuit reasoned, it was not necessary to determine whether wearing the T-shirt to school might disrupt the school environment.

The federal District Court in Massachusetts, responding to a dress-code dispute involving Coed Naked T-shirts, wrote, "[U]nless federal courts are to take on the task of assessing, each morning of the school year, the latest creations of the adolescent imagination . . . [,] the limits on vulgarity in secondary schools, assuming a general standard of reasonableness, are to be defined by school administrators, answerable to school boards and ultimately to the voters of a community."[70] This places the authority for defining what expressive conduct is acceptable in a school environment squarely on the shoulders of those who bear the daily responsibility for that school environment—the educators.

The Imprimatur of the School: *Hazelwood School District v. Kuhlmeier*

Fraser reduced some of the reach of *Tinker* by adding speech that is lewd, vulgar, and offensive to the types of speech that school authorities can ban without violating the First Amendment. Thus, in addition to student speech that school authorities reasonably believe is disruptive, school officials can ban speech that is patently offensive.

A third important Supreme Court case, *Hazelwood School District v. Kuhlmeier*,[71] added further restrictions on students' right to free speech in the school setting. *Hazelwood* involved the question of whether students have a constitutional right to make unilateral decisions about what appears in a student newspaper that was produced as part of a high-school journalism class.

In this case, student contributors to a school newspaper published as part of a journalism class contested the principal's decision to delete articles from the newspaper prior to its publication. The principal asserted that the articles were either inappropriate for the school's younger students to read or were not produced in accordance with established principles of professional journalism.

In their lawsuit against the school district, the students claimed the newspaper was an open forum, somewhat similar to traditional open forums such as streets and parks, which are commonly open to assembly and communication with minimal governmental restrictions. Since the newspaper was a public forum, the students contended, they enjoyed the constitutional right to determine what the newspaper should print without censorship by school authorities.

In deciding the case, the Supreme Court concluded that a high school's student newspaper is not an open forum as the students had argued. Rather, the newspaper, which was produced in a journalism class, formed part of the curriculum and was school-sponsored speech. Regarding such speech, the court ruled, "school officials may impose reasonable restrictions on the speech of students, teachers, and other members of the school community."[72]

Since the school was not an open forum for student expression, the school newspaper, as part of its curriculum (the speech of the school), was not a forum for indiscriminate student speech. The school, as a forum for speech, is "reserved for its intended purpose of creating supervised learning experiences."[73]

The *Hazelwood* court found that the school had authority over such school-sponsored publications as theatrical productions and "other expressive activities that students, parents, and other members of the public might reasonably perceive to bear the imprimatur of the school."[74] The Supreme Court held that educators do not offend the Constitution by exercising editorial control over school-sponsored expression "so long as their actions are reasonably related to legitimate pedagogical concerns."[75]

Deference to school authorities was given full weight when the Court reasoned, "We thus recognize that the determination of what manner of speech in the classroom or in school assembly is appropriate properly rests with the school board rather than the federal courts."[76] Consequently, "[a] school need not tolerate student speech that is inconsistent with its 'basic educational mission.'"[77]

Hazelwood's standard, allowing schools to censor school-sponsored expression based on legitimate pedagogical concerns, was applied by the Sixth Circuit Court of Appeals in *Morrison v. Board of Education of Boyd County*.[78] This case involved a high-school student who identified as a Christian who had a moral duty to confront others when he believed their behavior failed to measure up to his Christian teaching. The school's antiharassment policy and diversity training, he asserted, "chilled" his expression because he could be disciplined for speaking out against gays. He lost. The Court of Appeals upheld the district court's finding that addressing the issue of harassment based on sexual orientation through mandatory training "is rationally related to legitimate educational goal, namely to maintain a safe environment."[79]

Bong Hits 4 Jesus: *Morse v. Frederick*

The most recent Supreme Court student-speech case is *Morse v. Frederick*, sometimes known as the "Bong Hits 4 Jesus" case.[80] On January 24, 2002, the Olympic Torch Relay passed through Juneau, Alaska on the way to the Salt Lake City Winter Olympics. The route went past the Juneau-Douglas High School, and the principal allowed students and staff to view the event outdoors as part of a school-sponsored event. School supervision was provided.

Joseph Frederick, a student at the school, was late for class and joined some of his classmates across the street from the school. When the torchbearers and camera crew passed by, Frederick and several of his friends unfurled a banner proclaiming "BONG HITS 4 JESUS," apparently hoping they would be filmed by the television crew.

The banner could easily be seen from the school grounds. When Deborah Morse, the high-school principal, spotted the banner, she immediately crossed the street and ordered the students to stop displaying it. All of the students, with the exception of Frederick, complied. Frederick was ordered to the principal's office and was subsequently suspended. Principal Morse asserted that the banner advocated the use of illegal drugs, which was a violation of the school's policy. Frederick sued Morse and the school district in federal court, claiming a violation of his First Amendment rights.

A federal district court in Juneau, Alaska granted summary judgment to the school defendants.[81] Frederick then appealed to the Ninth Circuit Court of Appeals, which reversed.[82] The Ninth Circuit ruled that Morse had violated young Frederick's clearly established First Amendment rights and that he could sue Morse personally for money damages.

The case then proceeded to the US Supreme Court, which reversed the Ninth Circuit's opinion.[83] The High Court discussed the rulings in *Tinker*, *Bethel*, and *Hazelwood* but found them inapplicable to the case before it. The court instead looked to another line of Supreme Court cases to anchor its decision. The message of Frederick's banner could reasonably be construed as condoning or advocating drug use, the court said. (Frederick himself contended that the words were "nonsense meant to attract the television cameras."[84])

Consequently, the court turned for guidance to two prior Fourth Amendment student drug-testing cases: *Vernonia School District 47J v. Acton*[85] and *Board of Education v. Earls*.[86] In *Vernonia*, the Court had approved a school district's random drug-testing policy for student athletes; and in *Earls*, the

Court upheld a school district's random drug-testing program for students participating in extracurricular activities.

Vernonia and *Earls* both recognized that schools have an important governmental interest in stopping students from using drugs, the Supreme Court observed in *Morse*. Moreover, "Congress has declared that part of a school's job is educating students about the dangers of illegal drug use." The court pointed out that Congress had "provided billions of dollars to support state and local drug-prevention programs . . . and required that schools receiving federal funds under the Safe and Drug-Free Schools and Communities Act of 1995 certify that their drug prevention programs 'convey a clear and consistent message . . . that illegal use of drugs is wrong and harmful.'"[87] Indeed, the Juneau school board and thousands of school boards all over the United States had adopted policies to deter the illegal use of drugs among students.

Thus, in the Supreme Court's majority view as expressed by Justice Roberts, the special characteristics of the school environment and the strong governmental interest in stopping students from using drugs allow schools to "restrict student expression that they reasonably regard as promoting illegal drug use."[88] In fact, the Court asserted, "failing to act would send a powerful message to the students in [the principal's] charge . . . about how serious the school was about the dangers of illegal drug use."[89]

In concluding his opinion, Justice Roberts acknowledged the challenges that school administrators face. "School principals have a difficult job, and a vitally important one," Justice Roberts wrote.

> When Frederick suddenly and unexpectedly unfurled his banner, Morse had to decide to act—or not act—on the spot. It was reasonable for her to conclude that the banner promoted illegal drug use—in violation of established school policy—and that failing to act would send a powerful message to the students in her charge, including Frederick, about how seriously the school was about the dangers of illegal drug use. The First Amendment does not require schools to tolerate at school events student expression that contributes to those dangers.[90]

In short, the Supreme Court's majority opinion in *Morse v. Frederick* strongly affirmed the authority of school officials to ban student expression in the school environment or at school-sponsored activities that officials reasonably interpret as promoting illegal drug use. In fact, Justice Thomas suggested in his concurring opinion that students do not enjoy a First

Amendment right to freedom of speech while attending public schools.[91] The other justices did not join him in this assertion.

Although the *Morse* case dealt with a banner, not a T-shirt, this authority clearly includes the right to prohibit students from displaying messages on their clothing that celebrate or promote the use of illegal drugs. Moreover, although the Supreme Court's opinion did not mention the illegal use of alcohol, the opinion's reasoning at least implies that school authorities can prohibit student expression that celebrates or promotes the underage use of alcoholic beverages.

Thus, school administrators should make sure their school policies explicitly state that student expression that promotes or celebrates the use of illegal drugs or alcohol is prohibited in the school environment and all school-sponsored functions. Then, if "BONG HITS 4 JESUS" or a similar drug-celebrating phrase appears on a banner or a student's T-shirt, school officials can rely on that policy to take appropriate action to remove the offending message from the school environment without violating the First Amendment.

It will likely take a number of years for lower court decisions to determine the full implications of the *Morse* decision and to establish its place alongside the Supreme Court's three previous cases on the free-speech rights of students in the schools.[92] However, one commentator opined that *Morse* does not "mark a major doctrinal shift in student free speech."[93]

In summary, the Supreme Court has fashioned four tests that are used in student free-speech cases. Typically, courts review speech that is lewd, vulgar, or offensive using the *Fraser* standard. School-sponsored speech is analyzed under *Hazelwood*, and student speech that promotes drugs or illegal activities is reviewed under *Morse*'s standard. All other speech is reviewed under the *Tinker* standard to determine whether the student speech caused a substantial disruption or was likely to cause such a disruption.

Together, these four Supreme Court decisions make clear that a student's right to free speech in the school environment is not absolute, nor is it coextensive with the speech of adults. Students have the right to freedom of speech in school, but that right must be balanced with the legitimate interest of school authorities to efficiently and effectively provide instruction to their students.

THE PUBLIC SCHOOL AS A SPECIAL PLACE FOR SPEECH

The various courts have carved out a special niche in our society for the public schools. "Americans regard the public schools as a most vital civic institution,"[94] "perhaps the most important function of state and local governments,"[95] and "in most respects the cradle of our democracy."[96] However, in protecting that special place, actions that a student may take outside the schoolhouse gate often may be prohibited inside that gate. The Supreme Court, in the seminal student free-speech case *Tinker v. Des Moines Independent Community School District*, held that students do not "shed their constitutional rights to freedom of speech or expression at the schoolhouse gate."[97] "It is the appropriate role of the courts to help schools find the balance between its protective relationship and responsibility to all students and the expressive rights of developing individuals on the cusp of adulthood."[98]

Students have the right to freedom of expression at school, but that right is balanced by the compelling state interest to have public schools run in an efficient manner and to teach and preserve fundamental values. It has been asserted by some free-speech experts "that students will not learn the lessons of democracy if they cannot experience firsthand the freedom to make their own choices."[99] However, as the US Supreme Court noted, the First Amendment rights of students are "applied in the special characteristics of the school environment."[100]

A balance is sought between the student's rights and the preservation of the educational process.[101] "Free expression rights may be limited by policies that are reasonably designed to take into account the special circumstances of the educational environment."[102] The courts have somewhat curtailed student First Amendment rights by giving deference to school administrators' judgment as to what speech is appropriate in the context of the public school.[103]

Historically, the courts have been loath to intervene in the decisions of school boards unless it can be shown that the board acted in an arbitrary, capricious, or unreasonable manner. School boards have a substantial interest in creating and maintaining a safe and effective learning environment. And, concomitantly, they must protect the constitutional rights of their students.

Although students are considered "persons" and are therefore entitled to constitutional protections, these protected rights of speech and expression are limited. Chief Justice Burger asserted that "the constitutional rights of students in public school are not automatically coextensive with the rights of adults in other settings."[104] Forms of expression allowed by adults may be prohibited to children in a public school. Public-school children enjoy some measure of freedom of speech within the schoolhouse gates, but that freedom "is balanced against the need to foster an educational atmosphere free from undue disruptions to appropriate discipline."[105] Judge Posner, in a 2007 case involving a controversial T-shirt, stated the balance in the following manner:

> Prohibiting children from wearing to school clothing that contains "inappropriate" words or slogans places appropriately broad limits on the school authorities' exercise of discretion to maintain a proper atmosphere. Tighter limits, expressed in precise rules, would prevent them from responding to novel challenges well illustrated by the present case.[106]

The First Circuit Court of Appeals asserted, "The very nature of public education requires limitations on one's personal liberty in order for learning process to proceed."[107] Students have the right to freedom of expression at school, but that right is balanced with competing considerations including the speech of the school. A student's right to free speech is not absolute.

Our next chapter continues the discussion of the Supreme Court cases that structure the contours of student free speech. However, these cases are not education cases; they arose in different situations and have been applied to education cases involving student dress codes and primarily school uniforms.

NOTES

1. Clay Calvert, "Fringes of Free Expression: Testing the Meaning of 'Speech' Amid Shifting Cultural Mores and Changing Technologies," *Southern California Interdisciplinary Law Journal* 22 (2013): 547.

2. Nelda Cambron-McCabe, "Students' Speech Rights in an Electronic Age," *Education Law Reporter* 242 (2009): 493.

3. Thomas P. Brandt, Joshua A. Skinner, and Jennifer Kelley, *Schools as Incubators of Constitutional Litigation*. State Bar of Texas 25th Annual Suing and Defending Governmental Entities Course, Austin, Texas, July 2013. Available at http://txgovernmentlaw.org/Portals/0/Schools%20and%20Constitutional%20Litigation,%20Thomas%20Brandt,%20Joshua%20Skinner,%20and%20Jennifer%20Kelley.pdf.

4. Katherine Say, "Differing Viewpoints under the First Amendment: Students Versus School Authorities," *Oklahoma City University Law Review* 28 (2003): 906.

5. US Constitutional Amendment I. James Madison in his speech before the House of Representatives on June 8, 1789, supporting Amendments to the Constitution, proposed, "The people shall not be deprived or abridged of their right to speak, to speak, to write, or to publish their sentiments: and the freedom of the press, as one of the great bulwarks of liberty, shall be inviolable." Available at http://www.constitution.org/bor/amd_jmad.htm.

6. See, for example, Snyder v. Phelps 131 S. Ct. 1207 (2011) (protecting hateful speech at military funerals).

7. Palko v. Connecticut, 302 U.S. 319, 327 (1937).
8. Lovell v. City of Griffin, 304 U.S. 444, 450 (1938).
9. McIntyre v. Ohio Elections Commission, 514 U.S. 334, 357 (1995).
10. Alexander Meiklejohn, *Free Speech and Its Relationship to Self-Government* (New York: Harper, 1948), 91. See also Lyrissa Barnett Lidsky, "Nobody's Fools: The Rationale Audience as First Amendment Ideal," *University of Illinois Law Review* (2010): 839 (asserting, "It is generally agreed that a core purpose of the First Amendment is to foster the ideal of democratic self-governance.").
11. New York Times Co. v. Sullivan, 376 U.S. 254, 270 (1964).
12. See, for example, Texas v. Johnson, 491 U.S. 397 (1989) (burning the American flag as a protected form of speech).
13. United States v. Schwimmer, 279 U.S. 644, 654-655 (1929) (Holmes, J. dissenting).
14. Terminello v. Chicago, 337 U.S. 1, 4 (1940).
15. Cass R. Sunstein, "Academic Freedom and Law: Liberalism, Speech Codes, and Relevant Problems," in *The Future of Academic Freedom*, ed. Louis Menard (Chicago: University of Chicago Press, 1996), 96.
16. Harold J. Sullivan, *Civil Rights and Civil Liberties: Provocative Questions and Evolving Answers*, 2nd ed. (Saddle River, NJ: Pearson, 2005), 2.
17. Gilbert v. State of Minnesota, 245 U.S. 325, 332 (1920).
18. Texas v. Johnson, 491 U.S. 397, 414 (1989).
19. Ward v. Rock Against Racism, 491 U.S. 781, 791 (1989).
20. Erwin Chemerinsky, "Content Neutrality as a Central Problem of Freedom of Speech: Problems in the Supreme Court's Application," *Southern California Law Review* 74 (2000): 55–56.
21. Simon & Shuster, Inc. v. Members of the New York State Crime Victims Board, 502 U.S. 105, 116 (1991).
22. R.A.V. v. St. Paul, 505 U.S. 377 (1992).
23. Caroline Mala Corbin, "The First Amendment Right Against Compelled Listening," *Boston University Law Review* 89 (2009): 958–59.
24. Palmer v. Waxahachie Independent School District, 579 F.3d 502, 510 (5th Cir. 2009).
25. Linmark Associates, Inc. v. Township of Willingboro, 431 U.S. 85 (1977).
26. See Perry Education Association v. Perry Local Educators' Association, 460 U.S. 37 (1983) for a discussion of an open forum, a limited forum, and a closed forum.
27. Poulos v. New Hampshire, 345 U.S. 395, 408 (1953).
28. Chaplinsky v. New Hampshire, 315 U.S. 568 (1942).
29. Brandenburg v. Ohio, 395 U.S. 444 (1969).
30. Beauharnais v. Illinois, 343 U.S. 250 (1952).
31. New York v. Ferber, 458 U.S. 747 (1982).
32. Miller v. California, 413 U.S. 15 (1973).
33. Virginia v. Black, 538 U.S. 343 (2003).
34. Todd A. DeMitchell, Richard Fossey, and Casey Cobb, "Dress Codes in the Public Schools: Principals, Policies, and Precepts," *Journal of Law & Education* 29 (2000): 47.
35. Tinker v. Des Moines Independent Community School District, 393 U.S. 503 (1969).
36. Robert C. Post, "Between Governance and Management: The History and Theory of the Public Forum," 34 UCLA L. REV. 1713, 1774 n. 241 (1987).
37. Shelton v. Tucker, 364 U.S. 479, 487 (1967).
38. New Jersey v. T.L.O., 469 U.S. 525 (1985).
39. Goss v. Lopez, 419 U.S. 565 (1975).
40. Ingraham v. Wright, 430 U.S. 651 (1977).

41. Richards v. Thurston, 424 F.2d 1281, 1285 (1st Cir. 1970).

42. Bethel School District No. 403 v. Fraser, 478 U.S. 675, 681 (1986).

43. Ibid.

44. Tinker v. Des Moines Independent Community School District, 393 U.S. 503 (1969).

45. Ibid., 511. For a picture of the Tinkers with their black armbands, see Hudson, *supra*, note 12, p. 12. It is interesting to note that in the picture of Mary Beth and John Tinker, their black armbands had a peace symbol on them, a fact not discussed.

46. Ibid., 507.

47. Martha McCarthy, "Student Expression Rights: Is a New Standard on the Horizon?" *Education Law Reporter* 216 (2007): 15.

48. Tinker v. Des Moines Independent Community School District, 393 U.S. at 511 (1969).

49. Ibid., 513. The court cited Burnside v. Byars, 363 F.2d 744 (5th Cir. 1966), a case that supported students wearing "freedom buttons" on school property, holding that there was no disruption, thus students had the right to free speech.

50. Ibid. Justice Black's dissent lamented that the case was "wholly without constitutional reasons" and "subjects all the public schools in the country to the whims and caprices of their loudest-mouthed, but maybe not their brightest, students." Ibid., 525 (J. Black dissenting).

51. Ibid., 508.

52. Ibid., 513.

53. Ibid., 508. The use of the second prong has been spotty. The Third Circuit Court of Appeals wrote, "The precise scope of *Tinkers*' interference with the rights of others' language is unclear." Saxe v. State College Area School District, 240 F.3d 200, 217 (3d Cir. 2001).

54. Ibid., 513.

55. Newsome v. Albemarle County School Board, 354 F.3d 249 (4th Cir. 2003).

56. For a discussion of Confederate flags, free speech, and *Tinker*, *see* Richard Fossey and Todd A. DeMitchell, *Student Dress Codes and the First Amendment: Legal Challenges and Policy Issues* (Lanham, MD: Rowman & Littlefield, 2014), 53–80.

57. Palmer ex rel. Palmer v. Waxahachie Independent School District, 579 F.3d 502, 507 (5th Cir. 2009).

58. Morgan v. Swanson, No. 09-40373 (5th Cir. Sept. 27, 2011) (en banc) p. *17.

59. 478 U.S. 675 (1986).

60. Ibid., 678.

61. Ibid., 679.

62. Ibid., 682.

63. Ibid.

64. Todd A. DeMitchell, "School Uniforms and the Constitution: Common Dress in an Uncommon Time," *Education Law Reporter* 157 (2001): 7.

65. Bethel School District No. 403 v. Fraser, 478 U.S. at 682 (1986).

66. Ibid.

67. Ibid., 683.

68. Bethel School District No. 403 v. Fraser, 478 U.S. at 683 (1986). In Thomas v. Board of Education, Granville Central School District, 607 F.2d 1043, 1057 (2nd Cir. 1979), Judge Newman referred to Cohen's jacket, which had "Fuck the Draft" lettered on the back, citing to Cohen v. California, 403 U.S. 15, 21 (1971).

69. Boroff v. Van Wert City Board of Education, 220 F.3d 465, 471 (6th Cir. 2000), *cert. denied* 532 U.S. 920 (2001).

70. Pyle By and Through Pyle v. South Hadley School Committee, 861 F. Supp. 157, 170 (D.Mass. 1994).

71. 484 U.S. 260 (1988).

72. Ibid., 267.
73. Ibid., 270.
74. Ibid., 271.
75. Ibid., 273.
76. Ibid., 267.
77. Ibid., 266 (quoting *Fraser*, 478 U.S. at 685).
78. 521 F.3d 602 (6th Cir. 2008).
79. Morrison v. Board of Education of Boyd County, 419 F. Supp. 2d 937, 945 (E.D. Ky. 2006).
80. 551 U.S. 393 (2007).
81. Frederick v. Morse, 2003 U.S. Dist. LEXIS 27270 (D. Alaska May 27, 2003).
82. Frederick v. Morse, 439 F.3d 1114 (9th Cir. 2006).
83. Morse v. Frederick, 551 U.S. 393 (2007).
84. If Frederick's words were meaningless, could they constitute constitutionally protected speech?
85. 515 U.S. 646, 661 (1995) ("[d]eterring drug use by schoolchildren is an 'important—indeed, perhaps compelling' interest").
86. 536 U.S. 822, 834 (2002) ("The drug abuse problem among our Nation's youth has hardly abated since *Vernonia* was decided in 1995. In fact, evidence suggests that it has only grown worse."). Ibid.
87. Ibid., 408.
88. Ibid.
89. Ibid., 410. See Justice Alito's concurrence, "The special characteristic that is relevant in this case is the threat to the physical safety of students. . . . Students may be compelled on a daily basis to spend time at close quarters with other students who may do them harm. Experience shows that schools can be places of special danger." Ibid., 424 (Alito, J., concurring).
90. Ibid., 409–10.
91. Ibid., 419 (Thomas, J., concurring).
92. For example, see David Schimmel, "*Morse v. Frederick*: Did the Supreme Court Weaken or Strengthen Student Freedom of Expression?" *Education Law Reporter* 226 (2008): 557; Kathleen Conn, "The Long and the Short of the Public School's Disciplinary Arm: Will *Morse v. Frederick* Make a Difference?" *Education Law Reporter* 227 (2008): 1.
93. Bob Kennedy, "*Morse v. Frederick:* The Supreme Court Just Says No to "'Bong Hits 4 Jesus,'" *Education Law* 20 (2007): 6 (North Carolina Bar Association, Education Law Section). Available at https://educationlaw.ncbar.org/media/974994/10_2007.pdf. See also Melinda Cupps Dickler, "The *Morse* Quartet: Student Speech and the First Amendment," *Loyola Law Review* 53 (2007): 357 (writing, "By its plain language, *Morse*'s holding is narrow in that it expressly applies only to student speech promoting illegal drug use.").
94. Abington School District v. Schempp, 374 U.S. 203, 230 (1963).
95. Brown v. Board of Education, 347 U.S. 483, 493 (1954).
96. Adler v. Board of Education, 342 U.S. 485, 508 (1952) (Douglas, J., dissenting).
97. Tinker v. Des Moines Independent Community School District, 393 U.S. at 505 (1969). However, see Kristi L. Bowman, "The Civil Rights Roots of *Tinker*'s Disruption Tests," 58 AM. U. L. REV. 1129, 1130 (2009) (asserting that *Tinker* is a departure, in which "it was not a foregone conclusion that students had any affirmative free speech rights in public schools.").
98. Nuxoll v. Indian Prairie Independent School District, 523 F.3d 668, 676 (7th Cir. 2008).
99. David L. Hudson, *The Silencing of Student Voices: Preserving Free Speech in America's Schools* (Nashville, TN: First Amendment Center, 2003), 6.
100. Tinker v. Des Moines Independent Community School District, 393 U.S. at 506 (1969).

101. LaVine v. Blaine School District, 257 F.3d 981, 988 (9th Cir. 2001).

102. Martha M. McCarthy, Nelda H. Cambron-McCabe, and Stephen B. Thomas, *Public School Law: Teachers' and Students' Rights* (Boston: Allyn and Bacon, 1998), 114–15.

103. Denno v. School Board of Volusia County, 959 F. Supp. 1481 (M.D. Fla. 1997).

104. Bethel School District No. 403 v. Fraser, 478 U.S. 675, 682 (1986).

105. Bivens v. Albuquerque Public Schools, 889 F. Supp. 556, 559 (D.N.M. 1995).

106. Brandt v. Board of Education of City of Chicago, 480 F.3d 460, 467 (7th Cir. 2007).

107. Richards v. Thurston, 424 F.2d 1281, 1285 (1st Cir. 1970).

Chapter Three

Draft Cards and the American Flag

Noneducation Free-Speech Cases

> This connection between freedom of dress and a notion that control over our own bodies is essential to human dignity is part of why it strikes many of us as intrusive and unwarranted when someone tells us what to wear, how to cut our hair, or whether we can have a tattoo. It is as if the body is being taken over. [1]

In a time when Americans are concerned about civility in society, respect for legitimate authority, and security for schoolchildren, the debate about dress codes and uniforms has often been sharp. Do we as a society value or recognize the rights of students to wear clothes of their choice to school even if those garments are considered vulgar and offensive and filled with sexual innuendo, or are issues of clothing and appearance at school too trivial to lay claim to the limited resources of the courts and overstretched educators? In other words, do students possess a constitutional right of freedom of expression to wear clothes of their choice to school? A corollary question is what constitutes constitutionally protected expression. "Clearly, under most circumstances, one's choice of clothing is no more or less than expression of individuality and general sense of self."[2]

Students who argue that their clothing choices are constitutionally protected bear the burden of demonstrating that their clothing is "sufficiently imbued with elements of communication"[3] to receive First Amendment protection. For example, a student who wears an Aloha shirt to school would be required to persuade a court that the shirt conveys an expressive message that others would understand. Does every item in the clothes closet contain the seeds of protected expressive conduct? And, should the court system, with its finite and scarce resources, be used to adjudicate the dispute? We are reminded of a federal district court's admonition: if every time a citizen was outraged by the workings of a rather unimaginative bureaucracy he claimed a harm of constitutional dimensions, the courts would not just be crowded—they would be paralyzed.[4]

For example, in a 2006 case, a middle-school student sought to wear a red, white, and blue beaded necklace to school as a show of support for the troops serving in Iraq, including some of her family members. She was told that she could not wear the necklace because it violated the policy on gang colors and could be considered gang-related. She brought suit in federal district court alleging that the she was denied her right to free speech.[5] The court commenced its analysis by consulting *Texas v. Johnson*[6] and asking whether the necklace conveys a particularized message and whether there is a "great likelihood that the message will be understood by those viewing it."[7] The court did not find evidence that people viewing the student's red, white, and blue necklace would understand that it conveyed support for the troops. The court stated, "It is unclear at this point in the litigation whether anything about the necklace itself or the context in which Plaintiff wore the necklace gave any particular expressive meaning to it."[8] Merely intending to express an idea is not sufficient for the conduct to be considered speech.

However, while the majority of legal challenges to dress codes and school uniforms are based on the free-speech clause of the First Amendment, not all challenges have been based on free speech. Ariana Iacono enrolled as a freshman at Clayton High School in Clayton, North Carolina in August of 2010. Ariana, a member of the Church of Body Modification, brought suit requesting a Temporary Restraining Order (TRO) and a Motion for Preliminary Injunction in federal court against her school district. She sought to enjoin the school from enforcing its dress-code ban against wearing her nose stud.[9] The policy had an exception for religious reasons when compliance would impose a substantial burden on the exercise of a sincerely held religious belief. The religious exemption was not extended to Ariana's membership in her church; thus she alleged a violation of her First Amendment right to the free exercise of her religion. The federal district court granted the motion for the TRO asserting that the plaintiff would suffer harm to her Free Exercise rights if the code were enforced but the school district would not suffer a comparable harm. The school district settled the lawsuit.[10]

NONEDUCATION FREE-SPEECH CASES

The student free-speech tests fashioned by the Supreme Court in its four seminal decisions on the free-speech rights of students reflect the finding that the public school is a special place. Consequently, because it is special, the constitutional tests must address the school context. While the big four cases dominate student free-speech analysis, there is an emerging use of noneducation jurisprudence that is being employed with regularity in working through the balancing act of student free speech and school efficiency and effectiveness. In this chapter, we explore the noneducation cases, which have primarily been used in school-uniform cases but are also surfacing in dress-code cases.

These cases are important in school-uniform and dress-code cases because they focus on what constitutes speech in cases where students assert that nonverbal conduct and activities are entitled to First Amendment protection. If some activity is not considered speech, the protection of the First Amendment free-speech clause cannot be asserted.

The centrality of this initial analysis is found in *Tinker*. In *Tinker*, the Supreme Court first had to find that students have a constitutional right to free speech and then it had to decide whether the black armband was speech. The court decided in the affirmative on both issues. Wearing the black armband in protest of the war in Vietnam is a symbolic act "akin to pure speech."[11] We explore the most pertinent noneducation cases below, but first we review a dress code that used a noneducation Supreme Court case as the basis for its decision. The case essentially asked whether wearing sagging pants to school constituted expressive conduct.

Sagging Pants—Expressive Conduct?

In the fall of 1993, Richard Bivens was a ninth-grader enrolled at Del Norte High School in Albuquerque, New Mexico. During the first week of the semester, the assistant principal warned Bivens that he could not wear sagging pants to school. The school's dress code specifically prohibited students from wearing sagging pants, which school authorities associated with gang activity.

Despite being warned by school officials, Bivens persisted in wearing sagging pants to school. He received numerous verbal warnings and was subjected to a few short-term suspensions ranging from one to three days. In late October of 1993, he was given a long-term suspension. The suspension was for the remainder of the semester. Bivens, through his mother, who at one point acted as his attorney (*pro se* status), brought suit alleging a violation of his First Amendment right to free speech, expression, and association and his Fourteenth Amendment right to procedural due process.[12]

The court analyzed the contours of free speech and applied those principles to Biven's sagging pants. First, while not absolute, Judge Campos stated that freedom of speech "is a paramount guarantee."[13] Therefore, governmental constraints on the "communication of ideas must be measured against substantial and compelling societal goals such as safety, decency, individual rights of other citizens, and the smooth functioning of government" if government's restrictions on free speech are to prevail.[14] While public-school students enjoy some degree of freedom of speech within the schoolhouse gates, this right must be balanced against the need to foster an educational atmosphere free from undue disruptions.

> Judge Campos noted, "Not every defiant act by a high school student is constitutionally protected speech."
>
> Source: *Bivens v. Albuquerque Public Schools*, 899 F. Supp. 556, 560 (D.N.M. 1995)

If student's free-speech rights must be balanced against countervailing governmental claims of legitimacy, what constitutes speech is a threshold question. Not all conduct is labeled speech that is entitled to constitutional protection. The court in *Bivens*, citing *Tinker*, stated that wearing of a particular type or style of clothing is not seen as expressive conduct. The court noted that a two-part test was used to assess whether nonverbal conduct is "expressive conduct" and therefore entitled to protection under the First Amendment. The test was used by the US Supreme Court in *Texas v. Johnson* (1989); the American-flag-burning case.[15] According to the test, first, the actor must intend to convey a particularized message, and, second, there must be a great likelihood that the message would be understood by those who observe the conduct.[16]

Bivens asserted that his wearing of sagging pants to school was intended to identify his link with his black identity, black culture, and the styles of black urban youth. He argued that since wearing sagging pants is part of a style known as "hip hop," which is rooted in African American culture, it represents a fashion statement. And, if a style can be proven to have had its origins within a particular racial or ethnic group it becomes part of that group's identity. "Such intentional identification clearly must involve freedom of expression," he argued.[17] Granting that Bivens met the first prong of intentionality, the court was unpersuaded that he could prevail on the record before the court on the second prong. In other words, it was not clear that individuals would objectively recognize the message he intended to convey by wearing sagging pants.[18] If sagging is just a fashion trend of adolescents, then it would be devoid of a particularized message that would have a likelihood of being understood by others seeing the sagging pants.

The federal district court concluded that Bivens had failed to meet his burden of demonstrating that sagging pants is constitutionally protected speech. There was no showing that Bivens's intentional expression by wearing sagging pants was understood. Sagging pants is understood by some to mean gang association, yet Bivens stated that he was not a member of a gang. Others might view Bivens's sagging pants as a statement of black identity as Bivens said he intended. But others might merely see Bivens's pants hoisted to half-mast as conveying no discernible message except, perhaps, a fashion statement. With legitimate and competing views on what expression, if any, sagging pants conveys, it was difficult for Bivens to demonstrate that there was a particularized message in the sag.

The federal district court granted the school district's motion for summary judgment. If Bivens's sagging pants did not constitute speech, then prohibiting him from wearing pants that sagged did not abridge Bivens's free-speech rights.

United States v. O'Brien: Burning a Draft Card[19]

David Paul O'Brien burned his draft card on the steps of the South Boston courthouse in a symbolic gesture against the draft. O'Brien was attacked by members of the crowd. Several agents of the Federal Bureau of Investigation who were part of the crowd ushered O'Brien and his three companions into the safety of the courthouse where he was arrested, and he was later indicted, tried, convicted, and sentenced in federal court. His act violated the 1948 (amended in 1965) Universal Military Training and Service Act, which made it an offense to alter, destroy, or mutilate a draft card. He brought suit alleging that his free-speech rights were suppressed by the statute.

The Supreme Court faced the issue of whether O'Brien's conduct was speech. Writing for the court, Chief Justice Warren laid a marker for the analysis. He wrote, "We cannot accept the view that an apparently limitless variety of conduct can be labeled 'speech' whenever the person engaging in the conduct intends thereby to express an idea."[20] Even the intent to communicate ideas does not transform every act into expression that is protected by the First Amendment.

Furthermore, even if burning his draft card constituted speech, O'Brien had to prevail on the postulation that the statute's purpose was to suppress speech.[21] The Supreme Court asked whether the statute furthered an important or substantial governmental interest that is unrelated to the suppression of free expression and whether any "incidental" restriction was no greater than is necessary to meet the governmental interest.[22] The court found that the statute met a substantial governmental interest that was not related to the suppression of speech. Therefore, when O'Brien burned his draft card, he frustrated the governmental interest in maintaining its system of military service.

In other words, even if O'Brien's act of burning his draft card was expressive conduct, his act had violated a constitutionally valid, content-neutral regulation that was not aimed at the particular content of speech. Thus the government could prosecute O'Brien without violating his constitutional right to free speech. Chief Justice Warren wrote the opinion, joined by six justices, with Justice Douglas dissenting and Justice Marshall not taking part.

The *O'Brien* test essentially determines whether the disputed governmental regulation is justified by asking three questions. First, does the regulation further a governmental interest? Second, was the regulation adopted for reasons unrelated to the suppression of free speech? And third, is the government's interest in adopting the regulation greater than any incidental suppression of speech?

Federal courts have relied on *O'Brien* on several occasions to ascertain whether a school's dress code or school-uniform policy passes constitutional muster.[23] In those cases, courts have asked whether the dress code or school-uniform policy furthers a governmental interest (maintaining a proper educational environment, improving test scores, reducing violence, improving attendance, for example). The courts then ask whether the challenged regulation was adopted with the intention of suppressing student speech. Finally, the courts ask whether the regulation suppressed student speech any more than was necessary to further the school authorities governmental interest in passing the regulation.[24]

Indeed, courts that rely on *O'Brien* to decide constitutional challenges to student dress code or school-uniform codes generally make no reference to *Tinker*'s substantial disruption test. Whereas *Tinker* reviews a particular student expression to determine whether it creates a material and substantial disruption, *O'Brien* focuses on the challenged school regulation to determine whether it passes constitutional muster under the three-part test set forth above.

An example of the application of the *O'Brien* test in the context of a public school is found in a case involving a Kentucky high school. The Atherton High School-Based Decision Making Council adopted a school policy to support an environment that maximized student achievement. The council addressed a rising concern about student dress that might signal gang identification or promote violence. As a result, a dress code was enacted that limited clothing choices and prohibited clothing logos except the school's logo. Medallions and necklaces were also banned. Students brought a free-speech lawsuit, arguing that the dress code suppressed expressive conduct by limiting their clothing choices.

The federal district court applied the *O'Brien* test to the content-neutral dress code policy.[25] The court concluded, first, that school officials have an "important and substantial interest in creating an appropriate learning environment by preventing gang presence and limiting fights in school."[26] Second, the dress code had not been adopted for the purpose of suppressing student speech. Third, any suppression of student speech was incidental and outweighed by the school's goal of creating a safe and peaceful learning environment. In this part of its analysis the court took note of the fact that the dress-code policy "does not prohibit alternative and more specific student expression through badges, buttons and other means."[27] In other words, student speech was not totally stifled by the policy; there were alternative means for student expression. The dress code was reasonably related to a legitimate objective, the court concluded. Therefore, the dress code passed constitutional muster.

Spence v. Washington: The Peace Symbol and the American Flag

In *Spence v. Washington*,[28] the Supreme Court heard the case of a college student who responded to the 1970 invasion of Cambodia and student killings at Kent State University by affixing, through removable tape, a large peace symbol to the American flag (three feet by five feet). The student hung the flag upside down with the peace symbol outside his apartment window. His purpose was to associate the flag with peace instead of war and violence. His action violated a Washington statute forbidding the exhibition of the

American flag with attached or superimposed figures or symbols. He was convicted of violating the statute.[29]

The court, citing *Tinker*, noted that the symbol of the flag and peace sign were symbols of expression. "[I]t was a pointed expression of anguish by appellant about the then-current domestic and foreign affairs of his government. An intent to convey a particularized message was present, and in the surrounding circumstances the likelihood was great that the message would be understood by those who viewed it."[30] Consequently, the court cast the case as one of prosecution of an idea through an activity. It is interesting to note that the court found *O'Brien* to be "inapplicable" because no other governmental interest unrelated to expression was advanced or supported by the Washington statute.[31]

Spence meant to communicate his ideas by using the symbolism of the American flag affixed with the peace symbol. His act "was not an act of mindless nihilism."[32] It was the sort of communication through symbols that was a "short-cut from mind to mind."[33]

The *Spence* test states that for forms of expression to qualify as expression, and thus protection under the First Amendment, they must be "imbued with elements of communication" having a "particularized message" that would most likely be understood. The two-pronged test asked: (1) whether there was an "intent to convey a particularized message"; and (2) whether the "the likelihood was great that the message would be understood by those who viewed it."[34] Essentially, *Spence* established a test for the constitutional protection of the use of symbols as speech. It is important to note that *Spence* court found a lowered governmental interest in controlling expression because the speech took place on private property rather than on property over which government exercised supervisory control.[35] This may have implications for schools where school authorities do exercise control over student expression inside the schoolhouse gate that they could not exercise outside the gate.

However, *Spence* has been used in school settings to address "symbolic speech." An example is *Isaacs v. Board of Education*, in which a student, Shermia Isaacs, asserted that her headwrap celebrated her African American and Jamaican heritage (although she sometimes wore the headwrap on days when she was not pleased with her appearance) and thus should be exempt from the school's no hats/headgear policy.[36] The plaintiff student failed *Spence*; while Shermia may have intended to communicate about her heritage, her message was not particularized in that fellow students may not have understood her message. Some at the school became aware of her message after the controversy arose and some became aware of the intended message "based on what Shermia and her mother told them, not from their observation of the head wrap itself."[37] While the student intended it as a particularized message about her culture, others did not likely perceive Shermia's headwrap as containing that message.

It is worth noting that the *O'Brien* test was also applied. The court found that the no-hats policy passed constitutional muster because the school district had a governmental interest in securing an appropriate learning environment[38] and that the no-hat regulation's restriction on student speech was not greater than necessary to achieve the school district's goal.[39] Banning hats in a classroom was unrelated to the suppression of speech and Shermia had alternative ways to express her heritage.

Texas v. Johnson: Burning the American Flag[40]

The Republican National Convention was taking place in Dallas in 1984. During the convention Gregory Lee Johnson unfurled the American flag, given to him by a demonstrator, in front of the Dallas City Hall as part of a protest against the Reagan administration. With approximately one hundred demonstrators chanting and bystanders watching, Johnson doused the flag with kerosene and set it on fire.[41] There was no disruption, no injuries, and no breach of the peace following the flag-burning, even though several witnesses testified to being seriously offended by the sight of the burning American flag.[42]

Johnson was arrested, charged, and convicted of violating the Texas penal code, which made it a crime to desecrate a venerated object. The Court of Appeals of Texas affirmed the conviction, but the Texas Court of Criminal Appeals reversed, recognizing Johnson's speech as symbolic given the circumstances.

The US Supreme Court granted certiorari and heard the case. The Court began by asking the question raised in *Spence*, whether Johnson's expressive conduct constituted speech. Next the Court followed *O'Brien* and asked whether the state's regulation is related to the suppression of free expression.

First, the Supreme Court concluded, Johnson's burning of the American flag was related to a political demonstration that coincided with the Republican Party's renomination of President Reagan and was not a random act. "The expressive, overtly political nature of [Johnson's] conduct was both intentional and overwhelmingly apparent."[43] Second, the court held that government "has a freer hand in restricting expressive conduct than it does in restricting the written or spoken word."[44] However, in the instant case, the court asserted that government cannot appropriate specific symbols to only be used for the purposes designated by government. To allow government such authority "would be to enter territory having no discernible or defensible boundaries."[45] It was not the state's ends, to preserve the flag as the symbol of our country, with which the Justices took issue. Rather, the court disapproved of the criminalization of a citizen's conduct merely for using the flag to convey a message that was different from one that the state preferred. The Court did not believe that the special role that the American flag plays was endangered by the act of a solitary person.

> Our decision is a reaffirmation of the principles of freedom and inclusiveness that the flag best reflects, and of the conviction that our toleration of criticism such as Johnson's is a sign and source of our strength.
>
> Source: *Texas v. Johnson*, 491 U.S. 397, 419 (1989).

The flag is a symbol with great meaning for the majority of Americans. The Supreme Court called for more speech not less speech when it wrote, "The way to preserve the flag's special role is not to punish those who feel differently about these matters. It is to persuade them that they are wrong."[46] The individual's right to free speech encompasses the communication of "offensive and disagreeable" ideas.[47]

The Court's analysis took it through *O'Brien* and *Spence*. Basically applying *Spence*, the court in *Texas v. Johnson* asks two questions. First, is there an intent to convey a particularized message? If this question is answered affirmatively, the Court next asks whether it is likely that the message will be understood by the people who view the message.[48]

An example of the use of *Texas v. Johnson* in the context of the public schools is found in the New Hampshire case of *Governor Wentworth Regional School District v. Hendrickson.*[49] This case revolved around an ongoing dispute between two groups of students in a New Hampshire high school—the gay students and the "Rednecks." Tensions escalated between the groups when the Rednecks gave the Nazi salute and a "Seig Heil" response upon encountering members of the gay students group. The group retaliated by wearing patches to school depicting the "no" symbol, a circle with the swastika in the middle with a diagonal line through it. The principal was concerned about a further escalation of tension, which could lead to a disruption, and banned the wearing of the patches according to the school's dress code. A lawsuit was filed. At trial the court used *Johnson* to ascertain that the patches were symbolic speech and *Tinker* to establish a reasonable forecast of a material and substantial disruption. The patch was lawfully banned.

FREE-SPEECH TESTS AND WHAT STUDENTS WEAR TO SCHOOL

Students have challenged school rules banning clothing that identifies a professional sports team,[50] a prohibition against clothes that advertise alcohol,[51] a T-shirt proclaiming that "Drugs Suck,"[52] a ban against wearing Jeff Foxworthy (Redneck) T-shirts,[53] and a button depicting Hitler youth as a protest against a school's dress code.[54] And, as discussed above, a student asserted a constitutional right to wear sagging pants to school.[55] (A cultural expression, he argued.) Additionally, students have challenged school regulations requiring the wearing of a school uniform. In almost all of these cases, the complaining students have invoked their First Amendment right to free speech.

As we conclude this chapter, however, it should be emphasized that not all student clothing is veiled in constitutional protection, a fact that was emphasized in *Blau v. Fort Thomas Public School District*, decided by the Sixth Circuit Court of Appeals.[56] In that case, Amanda Blau, a middle-school student, wanted to wear clothes that "look nice on her" and that she "feel[s] good in."[57] Apparently, she wished to convey no particular message and her parents stipulated that the dress code did not interfere with any religious beliefs. The father's chief complaint, as well, was that the dress code inhibited her daughter's "ability to wear clothing that she likes."

Here, the dress code simply regulated the types of pants and tops students wore. Although Amanda argued that her desire to wear clothes that "look[ed] nice on her" was constitutionally protected, she lost her case.[58] Because Amanda could not demonstrate that her clothing choices were an attempt to convey a particular message that would likely be understood by others, her actions did not enjoy First Amendment protection.[59]

In addition, the Blaus unsuccessfully challenged the dress code on overbreadth grounds. They argued that the dress code impermissibly interfered with the First Amendment rights of others. To succeed on such a claim there must be a showing that the code suppressed a "substantial" amount of protected conduct. But before even reaching this question of "substantial" suppression of the conduct of others, the court first analyzed the dress code under the traditional *O'Brien* test for assessing restrictions on expressive conduct. Under that test, a restriction will be upheld if it is (1) unrelated to the suppression of the expression; (2) furthers an important or substantial government interest; and (3) does not burden substantially more speech than necessary to further that interest.[60]

In applying the test, the court found that the dress code's purpose was to create school unity and generally foster a school environment that enhanced student achievement. Therefore it was unrelated to suppression of student expression. The dress code furthered an important government interest, including the following: bridging socioeconomic gaps, focusing attention on learning, and reducing discipline problems. And finally, it passed the third prong of the *O'Brien* test in that it did not suppress more speech than necessary to further the school district's legitimate interests because the code applied only during school hours and students had other outlets of expression, such as writing for the school newspaper, or wearing buttons that expressed particular viewpoints.[61] In sum, because the dress code satisfied the *O'Brien* test, it could not be found unconstitutional under the Blaus' overbreadth challenge.

CONCLUSION: TESTS FOR DETERMINING WHEN STUDENT CLOTHING CHOICES ARE CONSTITUTIONALLY PROTECTED

The Supreme Court has issued four decisions on the free-speech rights of students in the public schools and three noneducation cases that lower courts often consult when deciding student-speech cases. Taken together, the Supreme Court has fashioned, albeit in an ad hoc fashion, a discernible pathway for determining the constitutionality of school restrictions on students' dress. Supreme Court guidance can be summarized as follows:

- Public schools are considered special places. They are not an open free-speech forum like a street or park.[62] Therefore, some restrictions on speech are possible inside the schoolhouse gate that would not be constitutional outside school premises.
- Symbolic expression is protected as pure free speech if it is intended to convey a particularized message and there is a high likelihood that those who view the message will understand the message. Symbolic speech is often considered expressive conduct, such as wearing a black armband in

protest, burning a draft card, or burning the American flag. Thus, protected speech can constitute more than just verbal expression.

- School regulations that pertain to student's choice of attire must support an important or substantial governmental interest that is unrelated to the suppression of free expression, and any "incidental" restriction must be no greater than necessary to meet the governmental interest.
- Schools can censor student speech that creates a material and substantial disruption, or that school officials reasonably anticipate will create a material and substantial disruption, regardless of whether the speech can be banned under other constitutional guidelines.
- Schools can prohibit student dress that is lewd, indecent, or vulgar. However, as illustrated by the conflicting decisions[63] involving the "I ♥ Boobies" bracelets, the courts are not always in agreement about what constitutes lewd or vulgar speech. In addition to the conflict in the courts, the US Supreme Court declined to review the *B.H. v. Easton Area School District* case,[64] thus leaving school officials with little direction about how to balance the free speech of students using ambiguously lewd speech and the need to control the educational environment.
- Schools may constitutionally regulate student expression that carries the imprimatur of the school so long as school authorities can articulate a legitimate pedagogical justification for their regulations.
- Schools may have to tolerate some student speech, but they do not have to affirmatively support all student speech.
- Schools can ban student speech or attire that promotes drug use. Such speech is not constitutionally protected in the school environment.
- Content-neutral regulations of time, place, and manner often survive constitutional scrutiny.

While *Tinker*, *Bethel*, *Hazelwood*, and *Morse* are used extensively in student free-speech cases, including dress-code cases, *O'Brien*, *Spence*, and *Johnson* are used in school-uniform cases and are gaining traction in dress-code cases. *Spence* and *Johnson* involve an analysis of symbolic expression to ascertain if it contains constitutional dimensions of speech. The tests essentially ask the same two questions. There is no discernible pattern for the choice of one of these tests over the other. Both are acceptable analytical tools in student free-speech cases that involve symbolic speech. *O'Brien*, however, does not focus on the speech. Instead it reviews the governmental interests served by the regulation or law and the impact of the law on speech.

Both cases were decided after *Tinker* and both arose out of nonschool criminal cases.

Our next chapter reviews the school-uniform cases. The noneducation cases discussed above will form the basis for the discussion.

NOTES

1. Gowri Ramachandran, "Freedom of Dress: State and Private Regulation of Clothing Hairstyle, Jewelry, Makeup, Tattoos, and Piercing," *Maryland Law Review* 66 (2006): 36.
2. Bear v. Fleming, 714 F. Supp. 2d 972, 983 (D.S.D. 2010).
3. Spence v. Washington, 418 U.S. 405, 409 (1974).
4. Swany v. San Ramon Valley Unified School District, 720 F. Supp. 764, 784 (N.D. Calif. 1989).
5. Grzywna Ex Rel. Doe v. Schenectady Central School District, 489 F. Supp. 2d 139 (N.D.N.Y. 2006).
6. Texas v. Johnson, 491 U.S. 397 (1989).
7. Grzywna Ex Rel. Doe v. Schenectady Central School District, 489 F. Supp. 2d 139, 145 (N.D.N.Y. 2006).
8. Ibid., 146.
9. Iacono v. Croom, No. 5:10-CV-416-H (E.D. NC Oct. 8, 2010), *2. The dress code stated that "no jewelry shall be affixed to a student's nose, tongue, lips, cheek, or eyebrow." Ibid.
10. Bridget Whelan, "Johnston Schools Settle with Student Suspended for Nose Stud." WRAL, June 6, 2011, http://www.wral.com/news/local/story/9691071/ .
11. Tinker v. Des Moines Independent Community School District, 393 U.S. 503, 505 (1969).
12. Bivens v. Albuquerque Public Schools, 899 F. Supp. 556 (D.N.M. 1995), *affirmed* 131 F.3d 151 (10th Cir. 1997).
13. Ibid., 559.
14. Ibid.
15. Texas v. Johnson, 491 U.S. 397 (1989).
16. Bivens, 899 F. Supp. at 560, citing Texas v. Johnson, 491 U.S. at 404 (1989).
17. Ibid., 561.
18. Ibid.
19. 391 U.S. 367 (1968).
20. Ibid., 376.
21. Ibid.
22. Ibid., 377.
23. See, for example, Palmer v. Waxahachie Independent School District, 579 F.3d 502 (5th Cir. 2009); Jacobs v. Clark County School District, 526 F.3d 419 (9th Cir. 2008); Blau v. Fort Thomas Public School District, 401 F.3d 381 (6th Cir. 2005).
24. Geoffrey A. Starks makes a case for the use of *O'Brien* in place of *Tinker* when the school policy is content-neutral, which is how a mandatory school uniform is often characterized. He argues that *O'Brien* is the better analytical tool because it applies the appropriate level of scrutiny and "it is better calibrated to confer the proper level of deference upon school officials." Geoffrey A. Starks, "*Tinker*'s Tenure in the School Setting: The Case for Applying *O'Brien* to Content-Neutral Regulations," *The Yale Law Journal Online*, August 30, 2010,

http://yalelawjournal.org/the-yale-law-journal-pocket-part/constitutional-law/tinker's-tenure-in-the-school-setting:-the-case-for-applying-o'brien-to-content%11neutral-regulations/ .

25. Long v. Board of Education of Jefferson County, 121 F.Supp. 2d 621 (W.D. Ky. (2000); affrm'd 2001 U.S. App. Lexis 18103 (6th Cir. 2001).

26. Ibid., 626.

27. Ibid.

28. 418 U.S. 405 (1974).

29. Three Seattle police officers observed the flag from the street. The officers arrested the owner with no disruption or altercation. There was no evidence that the flag attracted any attention on the street nor did Spence do anything to draw attention to the flag. Ibid., 406–9.

30. Ibid. 410–11.

31. Ibid., 415n8.

32. Ibid., 410.

33. Ibid. citing West Virginia State Board of Education, 319 U.S. at 632.

34. Ibid., 409.

35. Ibid., 411.

36. 40 F.Supp.2d 335, 336 (D. Md. 1997).

37. Ibid., 337.

38. The court found that the no-hats rule furthered the important governmental interest of providing a safe, respectful school environment that is conducive to education and learning. "[H]ats can (i) cause increased horseplay and conflict in the hallways, (ii) obscure the teacher's view of the student wearing the hat or view of the students sitting behind that student (and as a result can cause the teacher to miss signs of substance abuse or other health problems), (iii) obscure students' view of the blackboard, (iv) allow students to hide contraband, and (v) foster a less respectful and focused climate for learning." Ibid., 338.

39. Ibid.

40. 491 U.S. 397 (1989).

41. Ibid., 399. The protestors chanted, while the flag burned, "America, the red, white, and blue, we spit on you." Ibid.

42. Ibid.

43. Ibid., 406.

44. Ibid., 407.

45. Ibid., 417.

46. Ibid., 419. The court concluded, "We do not consecrate the flag by punishing its desecration, for in doing so we dilute the freedom that this cherished emblem represents." Ibid., 420.

47. Ibid., 414.

48. Ibid., 404.

49. 421 F.Supp.2d 410 (D.N.H. 2006).

50. Jeglin v. San Jacinto Unified School District, 827 F. Supp. 1459 (C.D. Cal. 1993).

51. McIntire v. Bethel School District, 804 F. Supp. 1415 (W.D. Okla. 1992).

52. Broussard v. School Board of Norfolk, 801 F. Supp. 1526 (E.D. Va. 1992).

53. Sypniewski v. Warren Hills Regional Board of Education, 307 F.3d 243 (3d Cir. 2002).

54. DePinto v. Bayonne Board of Education, 514 F. Supp. 2d 633 (D.N.J. 2007).

55. Bivens v. Albuquerque Public Schools, 899 F. Supp. 556 (D.N.M. 1995).

56. 401 F.3d 381 (6th Cir. 2005).

57. Ibid., 386.

58. Ibid., 388.

59. Ibid.

60. Ibid., 391.

61. Ibid., 392.

62. See Hague v. CIO, 307 U.S. 496, 515 (1939) (Roberts, J., opinion) (Justice Roberts writing, "Wherever the title of streets and parks may rest, they have immemorially been held in trust for the use of the public and, time out of mind, have been used for purposes of assembly, communicating thoughts between citizens, and discussing public questions. Such use of the streets and public places has from ancient times, been a part of the privileges, immunities, rights, and liberties of citizens.").

63. Compare K.J. v. Sauk Prairie School District, 11-cv-622-bbc, 2012 U.S. Dis. LEXIS 187689 (W.D. Wis. 2012), which found the ban on the bracelets to be constitution with B.H. v. Easton Area School District, 725 F.3d 293 (3d Cir. 2013), which found the ban unconstitutional.

64. Following the Supreme Court's March 10, 2014 denial of review, the school district ultimately agreed to a settlement to pay attorney's fees of $385,000. Kurt Bresswein, "Easton Area School District to Pay Attorneys' Fees in 'I (heart) Boobies!' Case." LEHIGHVALLEYLIVE, September 29, 2014, http://www.lehighvalleylive.com/easton/index.ssf/2014/09/easton_area_school_district_to_12.html .

Chapter Four

School Uniforms

Required Attire

School uniforms may well be a symbolic reform rather than a substantive reform. The jury is literally still out.[1]

POLICY AND POLITICS OF SCHOOL UNIFORMS

A policy[2] often solves a problem, clarifies a situation, and/or directs behavior that seeks consistency. Neither government nor public schools can address all of the issues that parents, citizens, and educators want solved. Consequently, the agenda-setting process narrows a wide range of conceivable policy issues to the set that actually becomes the focus of attention of government officials. So, how does an issue get on an organization's policy agenda for attention and resolution? The public agenda is small and crowded. The number of issue that partisans clamor to be heard is large.

John W. Kingdon's classic work on policy streams and policy windows provides a scheme for understanding how issues get on the public agenda and become public problems. He starts his work with the question, "How does the public know that an idea's time has come?[3]

Kingdon identified three streams that are constantly flowing and occasionally converge to open a policy window. First, there is a problem stream; gaining recognition for your problem is important. This often occurs when critical or prominent events or data/research help to focus attention on a problem. Second, there is a stream of proposals seeking problems to which they can become attached so that they can be implemented. The last stream is politics, the ongoing search to gather scarce resources through competition and coalition-building. This stream consists of political factors and actors who gain power and judge the political climate and mood, and voices of advocacy and voices of opposition. When these streams converge, a window of opportunity opens. When windows open, solutions can be grafted onto problems and a new policy is developed. These windows do not stay open long and advocates rush to take advantage of any opportunity to advance their policy agendas.

> Public school districts across the country have increasingly turned to the adoption of mandatory dress policies, sometimes referred to as "school uniforms policies," in an effort to focus student attention and reduce conflict.
>
> Source: *Jacobs v. Clark County School District,* 526 F.3d 419, 422 (9th Cir. 2008).

For example, after the massacre at Sandy Hook Elementary School, a number of advocates, or issue partisans, sought to attach their preferred solution to the issue of intruder violence in the schools. Gun-control advocates defined the issue as guns and pushed for policy responses that included bans on certain types of high-capacity ammunition clips and on certain types of firearms. Others pushed for hardening the school site by arming teachers and school administrators. Other issue partisans sought to define the issue as a mental-health problem and called for greater mental-health screening for persons seeking to purchase firearms.

Discipline, safety, good grades, and bright futures are things that all parents, community members, educators, and legal professionals want for their local public schools and their students (i.e., the problems). But how to fashion policies for a particular school to achieve these goals is the challenge. One proposal for enhancing academic achievement and school safety has been to require students to wear uniforms to school.

The federal government has inserted itself into the debate about the value of student uniforms in the public schools. The US Department of Education asserted that a safe and disciplined environment is a requirement for a good school and that "many parents, teachers, and school officials have come to see school uniforms as one positive and creative way to reduce discipline problems and increase school safety." In fact, the Department of Education even went so far as to state that "the adoption of school uniform policies can promote school safety, improve discipline, and enhance the learning environment."[4]

Furthermore, former President Clinton and former Secretary of Education Richard Riley supported the role of school uniforms in reducing violence and establishing an environment for students and adults that is conducive to learning.[5] Thus, school uniforms have been advanced at the highest level of the federal government as a positive strategy to reform schools—improving behavior, academics, and school climate.

Asserted Potential Benefits of School Uniforms

The US Department of Education offers the following potential benefits for implementing a school-uniform policy:

- decreasing violence and theft—even life-threatening situations among students over designer clothing or expensive sneakers;
- helping prevent gang members from wearing gang colors and insignia at school;
- instilling students with discipline;
- helping parents and students resist peer pressure;
- helping students concentrate on their school work; and
- helping school officials recognize intruders who come to the school.

Source: United States Department of Education, *Manual on School Uniforms*, (n.d.), available at http://www.ed.gov/updates/uniforms.html.

Nevertheless, in spite of the asserted benefits of instituting school uniforms as a strategy for improving student achievement, enhancing safety, and reducing discipline problems, uniforms have not surfaced as a major solution for educational problems.[6] While a growing number of schools have adopted school-uniform policies, they are far from universal in American public schools. In fact, between 2003–2004 and 2011–2012, the number of schools that have school-uniform policies in place has only grown from 13 to 19 percent.[7] For example, an e-mail communication sent by one of the authors (Todd) several years ago asked New Hampshire superintendents if they either had adopted a school-uniform policy or were contemplating the adoption of such a policy in the near future. While the response rate was somewhat low (only 32%), no responding superintendent reported the institution of a school-uniform policy and none had definite plans to implement one. One superintendent said she/he might consider school-uniform policy in the next two years, and another responded that the idea comes up every year, but there have been no serious talks about developing such a policy. One superintendent wrote that there are "too many other issues to deal with."[8]

Furthermore, Zernike, in a 2002 *New York Times* article, noted that schools in California, Utah, Florida, and Kansas had "abandoned" school-uniform policies.[9] Similarly, Mayor Bloomberg scrapped his plan to require school uniforms in New York City after reviewing a report on school uniforms that concluded that school-uniform policies had not "reaped benefits in other cities."[10]

Local politics, local conditions, and local perceptions often result in different conclusions about the wisdom of school uniforms. Thus, the fact that one school district concludes that a school-uniform policy would be beneficial does not mean that such a policy would be a good fit in a different school district.

> [T]he [Waxahachie Independent School District] noted that it had considered adopting school uniforms but decided not to do so, because it still wanted students to have some freedom to choose their clothing.
>
> Source: *Palmer v. Waxahachie Independent School District*, 579 F.3d 502, 505 note 2 (5th Cir. 2009).

SCHOOL UNIFORMS: THE LEGAL CONTROVERSY

The legal arguments for and against school-uniform policies are similar to the arguments that have been raised about school dress-code policies. Students who assert that a mandatory school-uniform policy abridges their First Amendment right to wear clothing of their choice generally argue that their clothing has some expressive content. In other words, students who challenge school-uniform policies or student dress codes are asserting that their clothing constitutes symbolic, nonverbal speech that is protected by the First Amendment. As discussed in chapter 3, the test used by the courts to analyze whether nonverbal activities have constitutionally expressive conduct were developed in several key Supreme Court cases that were decided outside the context of public education. At a minimum, courts have required individuals seeking constitutional protection for their nonverbal actions to show that their actions were intended to convey a "particularized message" and "that the message would be understood by those who view it."[11]

While the US Supreme Court has recognized that speech at school may be symbolic, it does not automatically mean that all choices of what to wear are symbolic expression. For example, as we discussed in chapter 3, Shermia Isaacs maintained that her decision to wear a headwrap in defiance of a school policy against wearing headgear violated her right to engage in symbolic speech that celebrated her African American and Jamaican heritage, but her argument failed in federal court.[12] Similarly, a federal district court in North Carolina upheld a principal's prohibition against wearing blue jeans to a graduation ceremony, finding no violation of the students' constitutional rights.[13] Blue jeans, in this case, did not involve discernible expression worthy of constitutional protection.

A second free-speech argument asserts that requiring students to wear a school uniform is tantamount to compelled speech reminiscent of the compelled flag salute of *West Virginia State Board of Education v. Barnette*.[14] For example, the plaintiff students in *Jacobs v. Clark County School District* argued that wearing a mandatory uniform forced them to convey a message of uniformity with which they disagreed.[15] This issue will be discussed below in *Frudden v. Pilling*.

As discussed in earlier chapters and as will be discussed in the next chapter, dress-code policies have mixed results when challenged in the courts. School-uniform policies define what is proper attire; all other attire is improper. A greater degree of certainty is achieved with a school-uniform policy, and educator discretion in deciding what is appropriate student dress is reduced as a consequence of that certainty. The amount of litigation concerning school uniforms is quite small in comparison to the litigation over student dress codes, but it is growing. As more schools adopt school uniforms, it is expected that the pace of litigation will likely grow rather than contract, absent a definitive statement from the US Supreme Court.

Before discussing the cases that specifically addressed the issue of whether a school-uniform policy violates constitutional rights, we will take a quick look at two cases related to school uniforms. These two cases are free-speech cases aimed at school uniforms.

Nonspeech Challenges Related to School Uniforms

Interestingly, two cases involving school uniforms were heard in federal court but the issue was not whether the mandatory uniform abridged free speech; the issue was whether students had the free-speech right to protest against the school-uniform policy. *Lowry v. Watson Chapel School District*[16] considered whether school authorities had violated the free-speech rights of students who wore a black armband to protest their school's school-uniform policy.[17] The protest bands were worn on the wrist, forearm, or bicep and did not cover up any portion of the uniform. The school administrators instituted discipline in response to the protest, believing that the students were trying to defeat the school-uniform policy. The students sued.

Relying on *Tinker*, the district court and the Eighth Circuit Court of Appeals found that the school had violated students' free-speech rights to engage in nondisruptive symbolic protest. The school district was permanently enjoined from "disciplining any student who wears a band substantially similar to the ones plaintiffs wore around the wrist.[18] The school-uniform policy was not disturbed by the ruling but the school district had to pay $37,500 in attorney's fees to the student plaintiffs.[19]

A second case involved buttons that students wore in protest of a school-uniform policy. Two fifth-grade students at two different elementary schools in the Bayonne School District in New Jersey wore buttons that proclaimed "No School Uniforms." In addition, the buttons displayed a slashed red circle with a background picture portraying Nazi-era Hitler youth in a military formation, all clad in identical uniforms.[20] The school district sent letters home to the students' parents stating that the pictures were offensive and did not constitute protected speech. The parents brought suit.

The court held that the buttons were not school-sponsored, and thus *Kuhlmeier* did not apply. Nor, in the court's opinion, did *Morse* apply because the buttons did not reference illegal drug activity. The court then turned to *Fraser*.

Analyzing *Fraser*, the court developed a narrow definition of lewd, vulgar, indecent, or plainly offensive speech. In the court's view, these terms related to the content of Fraser's nominating speech, which was replete with sexual innuendo. The court concluded that *Fraser* permitted schools to ban student speech that is more than inappropriate but less than obscene, a standard already accepted by the courts. This interpretation of *Fraser* limited the types of arguably offensive student speech that can be banned. The buttons, the court reasoned, did not reach the level of offensiveness that Fraser exhibited in his speech that was laced with sexual innuendo and profanity. The message was protected speech even though the court acknowledged that the buttons' reference to Hitler ("one of history's greatest miscreants") might be found by some to be offensive and in poor taste. [21]

Therefore, the court concluded that the protest buttons were not lewd or vulgar in the sense that they could be banned under *Fraser*. Nor, in the court's opinion, could the school ban the buttons under *Tinker* based on their potential for creating a school disruption. The buttons had created no disruption and there was no reasonable forecast of a disruption. However, the court instructed that if a disruption did occur as a result of the protest buttons being worn at school, then school officials could respond. As with *Lowry*, the school-uniform code was left in place. The students were allowed to wear their protest buttons; but in an odd ruling, the court determined that the student plaintiffs must be allowed to wear their buttons but they were not allowed to distribute the buttons at school. [22]

Up to 2014, all courts, including those that heard protest speech aimed at school-uniform policies, have upheld the constitutionality of school-uniform policies. The one exception, *Frudden v. Pilling*, [23] is discussed later in this chapter; it involved an argument that schoolchildren were forced to engage in compelled speech if they were required to wear uniforms that contained the school's motto. The state court decisions will be discussed first, followed by the federal court decisions. This chapter concludes with a discussion of the Ninth Circuit's decision in *Frudden v. Pilling*, which may be a game changer with regard to constitutional challenges to school districts' school-uniform policies.

SCHOOL UNIFORM CASES: STATE COURTS

Phoenix Elementary School District No. 1 v. Green (1997)

On September 6, 1995, the Phoenix Preparatory Academy, a public inner-city middle school, instituted a mandatory uniform policy. On the day of implementation, two students wore clothing that did not comply with the policy. One student wore a T-shirt with a US flag and logos stating "I support my country" and "America." The other student wore a T-shirt with a picture of Jesus Christ and the Bible along with the words "The School of Higher Learning." The students' parents informed the school authorities that their children would never comply with the mandatory uniform policy and insisted that they were entitled to opt out of the policy. The school district responded by transferring the students out of the Academy school to another school that did not have a mandatory common uniform policy. The following day, the parents and the students marched onto the Academy's campus, entered the classrooms without permission, and distributed literature to other students disparaging the dress code. Both sides sought declaratory and injunctive relief in the lawsuit that was triggered by these events.[24]

Consolidating the cases, the trial court started with the forum analysis of *Cornelius v. NAACP Legal Defense and Education Fund*, a noneducation case decided by the US Supreme Court.[25] *Cornelius* distinguished between a public and a nonpublic forum. A traditional public forum is a place or means of communication "which by long tradition or by government fiat [has] been devoted to assembly and debate." Street corners and public parks are typically perceived as public fora. Government's restriction of speech in a public forum must further a compelling state interest. Under *Cornelius*, government can restrict access to the forum "as long as the restrictions are reasonable and [are] not an effort to suppress expression merely because public officials oppose the speaker's view."[26]

Applying *Cornelius* to its analysis, the court found that the dress code regulated the medium of the message—choice of clothing—not the content of the message. It also found that the Academy was not a public forum and thus government could reserve the forum for its intended function, the education of students. Furthermore, the policy requiring a uniform was reasonable and an appropriate matter of concern for the school board. Finally, the trial court considered the interests of the entire student body and found that those interests outweighed the plaintiffs' freedom of expression rights.

The Arizona Court of Appeals disagreed with the appellants regarding whether the more stringent standard of *Tinker* applied to the dispute and agreed with the trial court that the *Cornelius* analysis was appropriate. The Arizona appellate court further agreed with the trial court that under the *Cornelius* standard the mandatory uniform policy's content-neutral restrictions do not contravene the First Amendment. The appellate court affirmed that a school is generally not considered a public forum. To ascertain the reasonableness of the regulation the court turned to *Hazelwood*, observing that school officials have great latitude to regulate activities that are reasonably related to legitimate pedagogical concerns.[27] The court concluded that the mandatory uniform regulation bore a reasonable relation to the pedagogical purpose of the school, which included the following considerations:

1. Promotes a more effective climate for learning
2. Creates opportunities for self-expression
3. Increases campus safety and security
4. Fosters school unity and pride
5. Eliminates "label competition"
6. Ensures modest dress
7. Simplifies dressing
8. Minimizes costs to parents[28]

Last of all, the Court of Appeals turned to the *Cornelius* analysis, which involved consideration of whether there were alternative avenues of student expression. The appellate court noted that the dress code provided students with such alternative methods of expression as jewelry, buttons, nonuniform days, and petitions. The court concluded that the school district's content-neutral mandatory uniform policy constitutionally regulates students' First Amendment speech in the nonpublic forum of their school. In the court's view, the policy regulated a method, not a message, and was reasonable in view of the pedagogical mission of the school. The school-uniform policy treated all speech neutrally, regardless of content, neither supporting nor opposing competing ideas.

This school-uniform case is one of first impression. The focus of the case was less on the speech of the student than on the restrictive power of the school. The court did not explore the contours of whether the selection of clothing meets the threshold of speech. It may be inferred from the court's use of *Cornelius* that student clothing has some protected communicative properties, but the extent and the margins of that speech have not been definitively charted. It may be that the constitutional issues typically raised with dress codes are sidestepped by mandatory uniform policies because a uniform policy is content-neutral.

Furthermore, the Arizona Court of Appeals used *Hazelwood*'s legitimate pedagogical concerns test to determine the school-uniform policy's reasonableness under *Cornelius*. The court also noted that the students have alternative methods of expression, including wearing buttons. The *Green* decision is conspicuous because the school-uniform policy that was challenged in that decision did not have an opt-out provision. Some have argued that an opt-out provision is necessary for a mandatory school-uniform policy to stand on constitutionally firm ground.[29] One legal commentator argued that the lack of a constitutional requirement for an opt-out provision would help to overcome a major hurdle against instituting a uniform policy in high schools.[30] According to *Green*, whether the student's clothing is speech is immaterial because the forum is content-neutral; all speech is treated the same, and government does not favor one idea over another.

Byars v. City of Waterbury (2001)

A school-uniform case in Connecticut raised a constitutional question separate from the free-speech argument, which has thus far dominated litigation over school uniforms. The Waterbury Public Schools approved a pilot program in 1997 to try out a school-attire policy that limited students to wearing clothing of prescribed styles and colors—basically a uniform. The following year the board of education adopted a school-attire policy as a pilot program. The policy in 1998–1999 school year provided an opt-out provision allowing parents to exempt their children from the requirements concerning style and color but not the list of prohibited items, which included wearing blue jeans. In 1999–2000, the opt-out provision was eliminated, making the school's student-clothing policy mandatory. The policy differentiated the elementary and middle schools from the high school. The high-school policy was less restrictive. Violations of the policy result in suspensions, with ten suspensions resulting in an expulsion recommendation.

After forty-nine suspensions for violations of the school-attire policy, Teshna Byars was expelled on July 20, 1999. She was assigned to an alternative school operated by the school district. She was allowed to wear blue jeans—the basis for the suspensions—at the alternative school, but her parents homeschooled her instead during the 1999–2000 school year.

Teshna, through her parents, brought suit against the school district in April of 1999.[31] The original complaint was amended in May 2000 after the school board eliminated the opt-out provision. Teshna claimed, among other complaints, that the mandatory uniform policy deprived her of her liberty protected through the Fourteenth Amendment to wear blue jeans. However, she did not allege that the uniform policy violated her right to free speech. Instead, she based "her claim on the fourteenth amendment's prohibition against actions which, in substance, rather than procedure, constitute a denial of due process of law."[32] The judicial analysis under a substantive due process claim is different from the traditional free speech analysis of *Tinker*, *Bethel*, or *Hazelwood*, and *Morse*.

> [T]he very nature of public school education requires limitations on one's personal liberty in order for the learning process to proceed.
>
> Source: *Richards v. Thurston,* 424 F.2d 1281, 1285 (1st Cir. 1970).

The court first decided which level of scrutiny was most appropriate for considering Teshna's constitutional claims. "When the right infringed is 'fundamental' the governmental regulations must be 'narrowly tailored to serve a compelling state interest.'"[33] Fundamental rights, the court opined, are central to our concept of "ordered liberty." Speech, voting, and childbearing are examples of fundamental rights requiring the strict scrutiny of the government's intended regulation. Under strict-scrutiny analysis, a court must find that the governmental action being reviewed must be necessary for the governmental agency to achieve its compelling state interest. Actions that do not involve fundamental rights are reviewed under a lesser standard. Under this lower standard, government's actions are valid if they are rationally related to a valid governmental objective.

Clearly, it is easier for governmental policies to survive the more lenient standard that only examines whether the policies are rationally related to a valid governmental objective. Strict-scrutiny analysis makes it more difficult for government to prevail because the action must be "necessary," a higher standard than rational; and the government objective being served by the policy must be compelling as opposed to merely legitimate. Government has a heavy burden when the courts employ the strict-scrutiny standard to a challenged governmental action. "The court in the *Byars* case found that there is no fundamental right to wear blue jeans to school, and that only the rational relationship test applies to the challenged regulation."[34]

The rational basis test was used to ascertain if the Waterbury school district's mandatory uniform policy was valid under substantive due process. The analysis started with a judicial review of the government's goal. The court found that the goals of the uniform policy were to "reduce disruption, taunting, theft and loss of attention to course work."[35] After considering testimony from the school's educators, the judge found that prohibition of blue jeans was rationally related to the stated goals.[36]

It is interesting and germane to our discussion that the court in *Byars* held that *Tinker* "approved the authority of school officials to regulate dress"[37] so long as the right to engage in specific fundamental rights such as political speech were not subject to unjustified regulations. In other words, the court asserted that the mere selection of what to wear to school does not necessarily implicate a student's right to free speech. This position not only supports mandatory uniforms but also student dress codes.

SCHOOL UNIFORM CASES: FEDERAL COURTS

Hicks v. Halifax County Board of Education (1999)

Aaron Ganues was just entering third grade at McIver Elementary School in the Halifax County Schools (North Carolina) when the case began. Aaron was a solid student with a good attendance record and no disciplinary infractions. That changed after the school board adopted a mandatory school-uniform policy in 1998. Catherine Hicks, his great-grandmother, had legal custody of Aaron. She voiced strong opposition to the policy, stating that there was nothing wrong with the colors khaki and blue in and of themselves; however, the policy took away all free will and required uniformity. She stated that the policy was "characteristic of the 'last days'" and "demonstrate[d] an allegiance to the spirit of the anti-Christ, a being that requires uniformity, sameness, enforced conformity, and the absence of diversity."[38]

At the outset, when the school-uniform policy was being developed, the school board knew that Catherine Hicks had religious objections to the policy and these objections were discussed by the school's ad hoc committee. The original draft of the policy had an opt-out provision for sincerely held religious beliefs. The opt-out provision was dropped after conversations with a number of parents from a variety of religious groups. The committee reached the conclusion that "the policy would not affect any religions in Halifax County and that "if it did, there would be a way that it would be a compromise."[39] They were wrong.

On the first day of school, Hicks stated that she would never comply with the uniform policy. Aaron was suspended for ten days but was given an opportunity to return to school. Hearings were held with a panel consisting of three teachers, which upheld the suspension. Aaron refused to wear the uniform and was suspended again. Ms. Hicks's meeting with the school board concluded with a vote to support the school's decision. Ms. Hicks withdrew Aaron from McIver Elementary School and enrolled him in Tabernacle Christian School. Aaron stayed for the remainder of the school year but left when the school ironically adopted a school-uniform policy. Suit was brought against the Fairfax County Board of Education, and individually against the superintendent and the principal.

The case was moved from the state district court to the federal district court. The plaintiff sought a preliminary injunction prohibiting the school district from applying the school-uniform policy to Aaron pending the trial. Essentially, the court held that the school district had the authority under applicable North Carolina law to adopt a school-uniform policy. The motion was denied and the defendant school board moved for summary judgment dismissing the claims. The court's analysis on the motion to dismiss follows.

The central issue in the case was whether the school-uniform policy placed an undue burden on the Hicks family's free-exercise rights, thus requiring an opt-out provision for religious reasons. In addition, Ms. Hicks alleged that the school-uniform policy violated her right to direct the upbringing of the child.[40] In the court's view, Ms. Hicks's assertion of two related constitutional claims required it to assert a "hybrid-rights rule" that would require the school district to justify its policy under a higher standard than mere reasonableness. Because Ms. Hicks had asserted a hybrid claim, the court subjected the school district's policy to strict-scrutiny analysis, the highest and most difficult test for government to meet.

The defendant school district argued that the school-uniform policy was a neutral law of general applicability that was not aimed at the suppression of Aaron's right to free exercise of his religion as espoused by his great-grandmother. At this stage, the school-uniform policy was not ruled unconstitutional, but the standard asserted by District Judge Britt did not bode well for its constitutionality. Under that standard, the school district was required to show that its policy was necessary to further a compelling governmental interest and that it was advancing that interest by the least restrictive means possible.[41] Nevertheless the school-uniform policy survived at least until the dispute went to trial.

On the eve of the trial the school district, possibly acknowledging the uphill battle it faced in meeting the strict-scrutiny test, settled. The school district amended its policy to allow for religious exemptions and paid for the cost of Aaron's private schooling. The American Civil Liberties Union (ACLU) hailed the settlement as a victory for religious freedom and students' rights. Deborah Ross, the executive and legal director of the ACLU for North Carolina, considered it a "bright day," asserting that "[n]o child should be denied a public school education for failing to comply with a school uniform policy that conflicts with his family's religious beliefs."[42]

In contrast to *Hicks*, a trial court in a different state later came to a different conclusion. In *Vines v. Board of Education of Zion School District No. 6*, parents brought suit alleging that an Illinois school district's student dress code violated their daughter's right to freedom of religion and freedom of speech and their own right to direct the upbringing of their daughter through their dress code.[43] These are fundamental rights. Nevertheless, unlike the *Hicks* court, Judge John W. Darrah did not consider the complaint to be a hybrid-rights case, and thus he applied a less stringent standard of scrutiny to the school district's policy.

The court found that the plaintiffs had not asserted any injury to their free exercise of religion. Furthermore, the court noted that schools are nonpublic forums and that the appropriate test for analyzing the dispute was *Hazelwood*, which merely asks whether the dress code is "reasonably related to legitimate pedagogical concerns."[44] The court accepted the school district's argument that the dress code was designed to improve the safety of the school and support the academic and social growth of students. "Accordingly, the Board's dress code constitutionally regulates [the plaintiff's] First Amendment free speech rights in the nonpublic forum of her school."[45]

Next, the court considered whether the school's student-uniform policy interfered with the Vineses' constitutional right to direct the upbringing of their child, the same claim that had been made in the *Hicks* case. The court used rational-basis test and not the strict-scrutiny test to analyze this claim. The court held that "parental rights are not absolute in the public school context" and, consequently, the dress-code policy was rationally related to the board's interest in fostering the education it presents to its students and improving safety.[46] The dress-code policy was upheld.

In both *Hicks* and *Vines*, parents brought suit seeking to find their child's school's dress policy unconstitutional. Both sets of parents asserted violations of the right to free exercise of religion and unconstitutional interference with their constitutional right to direct the education of their child. *Vines* brought forth an additional claim—violation of the right to free speech. In *Hicks*, the court considered the parents' claims to be a hybrid claim and subjected the school district's school-uniform policy to strict scrutiny. In *Vines*, the court reviewed the school district's policy under a more lenient standard, only asking whether the district's school-uniform policy was rational. In both cases, however, the courts upheld the policies.

Canady v. Bossier Parish School District (2001)

In 1997, the Louisiana Legislature adopted a law allowing parish school boards the discretion to implement mandatory school-uniform policies, provided that school boards gave the students' parents written notice explaining the uniform requirements. In the 1998–1999 school year, the Bossier Parish School Board required sixteen of its schools to adopt mandatory uniforms as a pilot study to determine the effect of the uniforms on the learning environment. After receiving favorable results, the school board implemented a mandatory school-uniform policy for all of its schools beginning in the 1999–2000 school year. The mandatory uniform consisted of a choice of two colors of polo or oxford shirts and navy or khaki pants.

Several parents filed suit in federal court seeking an injunction against the enforcement of the uniform policy. The parents claimed that the uniform policy violated their children's First Amendment right to free speech, failed to account for religious preferences, and denied their children's liberty interest in wearing the clothing of their choice.

The parents and the school board filed for summary judgment. The school board offered statistics showing a reduction in disciplinary actions and a rise in test scores after the implementation of the uniform policy. The court entered summary judgment for the school district, and the parents' appeal followed.

The parents in *Canady v. Bossier Parish School District*[47] put forward a two-pronged appeal. First, they argued that the trial court erred by concluding that the enforcement of the school-uniform policy did not violate their children's constitutional rights. Second, they asserted that the trial court abused its discretion by denying them additional time to conduct discovery.

The appellate court started from the proposition that before reviewing the specifics of the uniform policy it must first be determined whether a person's choice of attire qualifies as speech protected by the First Amendment. The court relied on *Texas v. Johnson*, a noneducation Supreme Court case discussed in Chapter 3 to decide this issue.[48] According to the test laid down in that case, an individual seeking First Amendment protection for nonverbal conduct must first show that the individual intended to convey a particularized message, and, second, that there was a great likelihood that the message would be understood by those who observed the conduct.

The Fifth Circuit Court of Appeals noted that the lower court relied on *Karr v. Schmidt*[49] and concluded that choice of clothing is a matter of taste or style and is not afforded First Amendment protection.[50] While *Karr* focused on hair length and communicative content, the district court deemed hair length and clothing as essentially the same for purposes of constitutional protection. The appellate court disagreed. It found that while a "person's choice of clothing may be predicated solely on considerations of style and comfort, an individual's choice of attire also may be endowed with sufficient levels of intentional expression to elicit First Amendment shelter."[51] Conduct coupled with communicative intent raises First Amendment concerns, the court opined.

In essence, the court took an expansive view regarding a person's choice of clothing, concluding that such choices may be infused with expressive elements. Words printed on clothing qualify as pure speech and are protected under the First Amendment, the court pointed out. In addition, clothing may symbolize ethnic heritage or religious beliefs. Citing *Tinker*'s armband as authority, the court also argued that color patterns or styles may be speech if worn with intent to express a particular message. "The choice to wear clothing as a symbol of an opinion or cause is undoubtedly protected under the First Amendment if the message is likely to be understood by those intended to view it."[52]

The court further observed that students often choose attire with intent to signify the social group to which they belong and to communicate their attitude toward society in general and the school environment in particular. The audience for the message need not be adults, which may hold the message as of little value. However, "it has a considerable [effect], whether positive or negative, on a young person's social development."[53] The court concluded that expression of one's identity and group affiliation through choice of clothing may meet the threshold for protected speech. Accordingly, the Court of Appeals disagreed with the district court's "blanket assertion that, like the length of a male student's hair, clothing does not contain sufficient communicative intent."[54]

The Fifth Circuit offered several cautions regarding an overexpansive reading of its analysis lest it appear that the court intended to imbue all clothing choices with expressive protection. First, in a footnote, the court stated that "[w]e do not conclude that every choice of clothing expresses a particularized message."[55] Second, the court stated that even if the forms of expressive conduct are protected speech, that protection is not absolute, "especially in the public school setting." The public school was carved out as a niche occupying a special place in First Amendment protection. The court noted that educators have an essential role in regulating school affairs and establishing appropriate standards of conduct, and these obligations must be balanced with the civil liberties of students. Citing the Supreme Court's decision in *Hazelwood*, the Fifth Circuit wrote, "School boards, not federal courts, have the authority to decide what constitutes appropriate behavior and dress in public schools."[56]

The *Canady* court found that the facts of the case did not readily conform to any of the three categories addressed by the Supreme Court—*Tinker*, *Bethel*, and *Hazelwood*. (*Morse* had not yet been decided at the time of the Fifth Circuit's opinion but it seems unlikely that the Fifth Circuit would have found *Morse* relevant, even if the *Morse* decision had been available to it.) In the Fifth Circuit's view, the Bossier Parish School Board's mandatory uniform policy was viewpoint-neutral on its face and as applied. Thus, the facts in *Canady* were different from the facts in *Tinker*, where the school regulation targeted the viewpoint of the antiwar movement.

Also, unlike *Fraser*, the students in the *Canady* case were not punished for lewd, obscene, or patently offensive words or pictures. Finally, a student's choice to wear certain apparel to school was not a school-sponsored activity or related to the school curriculum, making the case before the Fifth Circuit quite different from the issues considered in *Hazelwood*.

Rejecting the three major student free-speech Supreme Court cases, the Fifth Circuit was left with the need to fashion an appropriate test. The court began by noting that a student's clothing choices constitute personal expression that happens to occur on school premises and that the school board's uniform policy was unrelated to any particular viewpoint. Thus, in the court's view, a level of scrutiny should apply to the school-uniform dispute that is higher than the standard in *Hazelwood*, but less stringent than the school official's burden in *Tinker*. The court adopted the *O'Brien* intermediate scrutiny test.

Under the *O'Brien* analysis, a mandatory uniform policy will pass constitutional scrutiny if it furthers an important or substantial government interest, if the interest is unrelated to the suppression of student expression, and if the incidental restrictions on First Amendment activities are no more than necessary to facilitate that interest.

First, the Fifth Circuit concluded that improving the educational process is undoubtedly an important governmental interest furthered by the uniform policy. The court cited school board statistics showing that one year after implementing the school uniform policy in several schools, "discipline problems drastically decreased and overall test scores improved."[57] Second, the court asserted that the purpose behind the school uniform policy—reduction in discipline problems and improved test scores—was unrelated to the suppression of student speech. Second, the court noted, while students were restricted from wearing clothing of their choice at school, they remained free to wear what they wanted after school. Third, students were also free to express their views through other means throughout the school day. The Fifth Circuit Court of Appeals did not state what those speech media might be. In a two-paragraph application of the *O'Brien* test, the court affirmed the district court's order granting summary judgment in favor of the Bossier Parish School Board.

In a similar case, *Long v. Board of Education of Jefferson County*,[58] involving a restrictive dress code rather than a uniform policy, a federal district court utilized the *O'Brien* test to find a school district's dress regulation to be on constitutionally firm ground. In an apparent departure from *Tinker*, the court stated it is "unnecessary to require the School to show that the Dress Code was necessary to stop an actual disruption."[59] As with *Canady*, the *Long* court distinguished the application of *Tinker*, *Fraser*, and *Hazelwood* and opted for the "less stringent" standard of *O'Brien*. The court concluded that the dress code was reasonable and therefore did not violate the plaintiffs' First Amendment rights.

Littlefield v. Forney Independent School District (2001)

The Forney Independent School District, acting under authority provided in the Texas Education Code, passed a mandatory school-uniform policy in 1999. Prior to the implementation of the code, the school district had a dress code that prohibited certain types of clothing deemed unsafe, immodest, or otherwise inimical to the educational process. There was no reported finding that the dress-code policy was ineffective. Nevertheless, the uniform policy was adopted to promote school spirit and school values, promote the decorum of a school as a place of order and work, and promote respect for authority. It was also asserted that the uniform policy was designed to decrease socioeconomic tensions, to increase attendance, and to reduce dropout rates. The relationship between these outcomes and wearing uniforms was not stated. Failure to comply with the uniform policy resulted in disciplinary action up to expulsion.

Suit was brought in 2000 against the policy claiming a violation of students' free-speech rights. The plaintiffs argued that the uniform policy acted as a form of coerced speech conveying a state-approved message and that it constituted a prior restraint that prevented students from expressing their own chosen messages through their attire.[60]

The defendant school district asserted that a student's choice of clothing is not expressive conduct protected by the First Amendment. The school district also contended "that the wearing of school uniforms does not convey a sufficiently particularized message to be considered coerced speech."[61]

Under *Canady*, discussed above, a person's choice of clothing is infused with intentional expression and may amount to protected speech.[62] Also following *Canady*, the Fifth Circuit Court of Appeals applied the *O'Brien* test. The court first easily found that that the school district had the power to implement a uniform policy pursuant to state law. "Second, improving the educational process is undoubtedly an important and substantial interest of Forney and the school board."[63] Third, the plaintiffs did not establish that the school district's goal was to suppress expression. Consequently, the Fifth Circuit found that the mandatory uniform policy "survives First Amendment scrutiny under the *O'Brien* test."[64] Thus, the school-uniform policy was found to be constitutional.

Lowry v. Watson Chapel School District (2007)

We return to the *Lowry* discussion alluded to above. Watson Chapel School District adopted a mandatory school-uniform policy in the spring of 2006 to promote "equal educational opportunity though economic access to appropriate and orderly, uniform apparel standards for students."[65] A number of students and parents opposed the policy. On October 6, 2006, several students wore black armbands reminiscent of *Tinker* to protest the policy. The students did not wear the black armbands over any part of their school uniform; and thus their conduct was in accordance with the policy, which allowed students to wear jewelry, including wristbands, as long as they were not worn over any part of the school uniform. The students were disciplined and a suit in federal court was filed four days later. The court granted the students' motion for a preliminary injunction. On February 22, 2007, the plaintiffs amended their complaint, adding allegations that the school-uniform policy violated their freedom of expression in that it constituted a prior restraint on speech, that enforcement of the policy violated students' due process rights, and that the student literature policy violated students' right to freedom of expression.[66]

The federal district court began its analysis acknowledging that neither the Supreme Court nor the Eighth Circuit had decided a school-uniform or dress-code case on First Amendment grounds. Lacking precedent, the court turned to the Sixth Circuit's decision in *Blau v. Fort Thomas Public School District*[67] and the Fifth Circuit's decision in *Littlefield v. Forney Independent School District*, discussed earlier.[68]

First, utilizing the three-prong *O'Brien* test, the court found that the school-uniform policy was adopted for reasons unrelated to the suppression of expression. Furthermore, while students were required to wear the school uniform while at school, they were "absolutely free of the school uniform policy" after school, on the weekend, during holidays, and during vacations.[69] They could wear whatever they wanted during those times, expressing themselves in any way they desired.

Turning to the second prong of the *O'Brien* test, the court asked whether the policy furthered an important governmental interest. The court concluded that indeed the policy was intended to further important governmental interests such as bridging socioeconomic gaps between families in the school district, focusing attention on learning rather than fashion, and improving school security.

Regarding *O'Brien*'s third prong, the court concluded that the policy did not burden more speech than necessary. In the court's view, the policy was not adopted as a pretext to suppress opinion and the uniform "requirement [did] not bar the 'important' personal inter-communication among students' necessary to an effective educational process."[70] In other words, the school-uniform policy did not foreclose all the means of communication available to students while they were in school. Having met the standards of *O'Brien*, the court concluded, "The school uniform policy adopted by the Watson Chapel School District contravenes no provision of the United States Constitution."[71]

Derry v. Marion Community Schools (2008)

One of the arguments advanced by school-uniform advocates is that a school uniform will save parents money in that they will not have to buy a lot of expensive clothes in response to the designer wars that are often waged among students in the schools. This tenet was tested in an Indiana case. Soon after a school-uniform policy was adopted for McCulloch Middle School, parents brought suit seeking a preliminary injunction against its implementation on the grounds that the costs of the uniforms would place an undue burden on their family, thus violating due process and equal protection.[72] The parents did not pursue a free-speech argument.

The school-uniform policy specified the colors and types of clothes that students could wear, thus restricting students' clothing choices.[73] Exceptions were made for physical conditions or religious affiliations. The school administration conducted research on school uniforms and found that uniforms, among other findings, helped to prevent gang-related clothing issues, focused students more on learning, and that "uniforms helped to level the playing field between students who can and cannot afford brand name clothing."[74]

The parents of two middle-school students preferred to buy new clothes for the children and planned to purchase five sets of uniforms for each child so they could have a different uniform for each day of the week. Their equal-protection argument asserted that the uniform policy was not rationally related to improving education or reducing disciplinary problems. Because some students had opt-out provisions, the parents argued that it did not make sense to have the two groups intermingle at school functions and extracurricular events. They asserted their fundamental right to make decisions regarding the "care, custody, and control of their children."[75] This was the same argument unsuccessfully asserted by the cases discussed previously (*Blau v. Fort Thomas Public School District* and *Littlefield v. Forney Independent School District*).

In deciding the case, the court used the rational-basis analysis and not a strict-scrutiny analysis reserved for suspect classifications and fundamental interests. The federal district court held that parents "do not have a fundamental right to direct the dress code and school uniform policy."[76] McCulloch Middle School, the court found, was a low-performing school that had not shown adequate yearly progress in the previous five years and that in the prior year it had logged three thousand disciplinary referrals. The court concluded that the school was acting rationally to address its academic and disciplinary problems and that trying a school uniform "experiment" was tailored to address those problems. In the court's opinion, the nexus between the policy and goals need not be perfect.

Finding a rational basis for the school-uniform policy, the court held that parents were not required to purchase a minimum amount of uniforms. Nor did the policy require the uniforms be purchased from either expensive or discount stores. In addition, parents could access the free-uniform program. Therefore, parents retained considerable control over the costs of the school uniforms. The equal-protection claim failed, and because it failed, the due-process claim failed as well. In short, the school-uniform policy withstood constitutional scrutiny.

Jacobs v. Clark County School District (2008)

The Clark County School District adopted Regulation #5131 creating a dress code for all of its students. The regulation also allowed individual schools to adopt a more stringent school-uniform code. The school-uniform policies were to be established "for the purpose[s] of increasing student achievement, promoting safety, and enhancing a positive school environment."[77]

The Liberty High School uniform regulation required all students to wear solid khaki-colored bottoms and solid-colored polo, tee, or button-down shirts (blue, red, or white) with or without Liberty logos. Kimberly Jacobs, an eleventh grader at Liberty High School, violated the school district's policy five times, resulting in twenty-five days of suspension. The school provided educational services to Kimberly during the suspensions.[78] Kimberly brought suit against the school district seeking declaratory relief that the school-uniform policy violated her free-speech rights among other allegations. She asked that her disciplinary records be expunged, and that she be awarded appropriate damages. Kimberly won her preliminary injunction but moved to another school district. Concerned about the viability of the lawsuit, a number of students and their parents joined the suit seeking declaratory and injunctive relief and appropriate damages. However, on summary judgment, the defendant school district prevailed.

On appeal, the plaintiffs alleged that the implementation of the school-uniform policy prevented them from engaging in pure speech[79] and expressive conduct,[80] and that it compelled them "to 'speak' in a particular manner."[81]

In considering these claims, the court began with a review of whether *Tinker*'s "substantial disruption" test applied to a school-uniform case, which involved content-neutral regulations on expressive conduct rather than pure speech. The Ninth Circuit Court of Appeals found that the stricter standard of *Tinker*'s substantial-interference test applied to pure speech but not to expressive conduct, citing the Fifth Circuit's decision in *Canady*. Like the Fifth Circuit, the Ninth Circuit selected the intermediate scrutiny test utilized in *O'Brien*. Nothing in the school-uniform regulation, the court opined, was directed at suppressing "the expression of particular ideas,[82] or to manipulate the public debate through coercion rather than persuasion."[83] Instead, the regulation was directed at (1) promoting safety by "reducing the ability to hide weapons, drugs, or alcohol; (2) allowing students and staff to focus more attention on increasing student achievement; (3) eliminating dress differences that emphasize different income levels; and (4) simplifying daily school preparation and maintenance for families."[84] The appellate court found that the school-uniform policy was content-neutral "despite [the] allowances for clothing containing school logos."[85]

As previously explained, the intermediate scrutiny test of *O'Brien* involves a three-step analysis.[86] As applied to the Clark County School District mandatory school-uniform policy, the court found that the policy furthered important governmental interests of "increasing student achievement, promoting safety, and enhancing a positive school environment."[87] The second prong of *O'Brien*'s intermediate scrutiny analysis asks whether the school district's interests are unrelated to the suppression of free expression. The court asserted that on their face, the "District's goals have nothing to do with quelling speech or limiting expression."[88] The district's policy, the court argued, is not a pretext "for an underlying desire to limit free speech."[89] *O'Brien*'s third prong requires that the school-uniform policy not restrict more speech than necessary. A school uniform restricts the clothing choices of students, which limits students' ability to express themselves by way of their choice of clothes that they wear at school. However, the Ninth Circuit pointed out, students retained the ability to express themselves through the school day via other means such as having verbal conversations, publishing articles in the school newspaper, and joining student clubs. Furthermore, students could wear what they wanted when school was not in session.

In short, the Clark County School District mandatory uniform policy withstood intermediate scrutiny under the three-pronged test set forth in *O'Brien*. Therefore, the school district had not abridged students' free speech rights with its student-uniform policy.

The plaintiff's last allegation was that the school-uniform policy compelled students to express support for the school district's message of conformity. The plaintiff argued that wearing a uniform conveys symbolic messages of conformity and community affiliation.[90] The court disagreed, finding it unlikely that a person viewing a student's uniform would understand it to be a message of conformity.

The Ninth Circuit Court of Appeals upheld the district court's grant of summary judgment in favor of the school district.[91] School uniforms prevailed again.

Until 2014, school districts consistently had their school-uniform policies upheld by the courts. But a 2014 case that arose in Nevada changed this unbroken line of victories.

Frudden v. Pilling (2014)

Roy Gomm Elementary School in Reno, Nevada passed a school-uniform policy in May of 2011, with two-thirds of the families voting to approve the mandatory school-uniform policy.[92] Students were required to wear red or navy polo-style shirts and tan or khaki bottoms during school hours. Students were not allowed to alter the uniform. The uniform shirts had the Roy Gomm logo of a gopher with the words "Roy Gomm Elementary School" and the school motto above it—"Tomorrow's Leaders." The policy contained an exemption that allowed students to wear uniforms from nationally recognized youth organizations such as the Boy Scouts or Girl Scouts in lieu of the school's approved student uniform.

In early fall, soon after the policy was implemented, the Frudden children (a fifth-grade boy and a third-grade girl) did not wear the required uniform; no action was taken by the school. Approximately two weeks later, they wore uniforms from the Youth Soccer Organization. The students were asked to change because there was no meeting of the soccer club on the day the students wore their soccer uniforms to school, nor was a soccer practice scheduled for that day.

The next day, the Frudden children wore their soccer uniforms again. And on the following day, September 14, 2011, the fifth-grade boy wore his school uniform shirt inside out so that the logo was not visible. He was asked to turn it right-side-out and he complied. The Fruddens then brought suit.[93]

Two Supreme Court cases were key to the Ninth Circuit's discussion of the school uniform's "Tomorrow's Leaders" logo, which was framed by two constitutional concepts. First, in *Riley v. National Federation of the Blind*, the Supreme Court had ruled that the right to speak connotes a complimentary right to refrain from speaking.[94] Second, in a teachers' union case, the Supreme Court had written, "at the heart of the First Amendment is the notion that an individual should be free to believe as he will, and that in a free society one's beliefs should be shaped by his mind and his conscience rather than coerced by the State."[95] In other words, concomitant with the right to speak is the right not to be compelled to speak.

Law is concerned with external behavior, and not with the inner life of a man.

Source: *West Virginia Board of Education v. Barnette*, 319 U.S. 624, 655 (1943) (Frankfurter, J., dissenting).

The federal district court, acting in response to the defendant school district's motion, dismissed the case, finding the school-uniform policy to be constitutional. Among other findings,[96] the court found the motto[97] with the picture of a gopher, while slightly complex, to be innocuous. The district court concluded that there was no meaningful risk that the students would be conveying a message of conformity. The plaintiffs alleged the school uniform compelled students to wear an expressive statement that was not viewpoint-neutral, "and that the very fact of wearing a uniform compel[led] the expression of support for group affiliation."[98] But the district court rejected this argument and granted the defendant school district's motion to dismiss. The Fruddens appealed.

On appeal the Ninth Circuit began its analysis by stating that the "right of freedom of thought protected by the First Amendment against state action includes both the right to speak freely and the right to refrain from speaking at all."[99] In *West Virginia Board of Education v. Barnette*,[100] the court noted, the Supreme Court had ruled that a state board of education was prohibited by the First Amendment from requiring schoolchildren to participate in the Pledge of Allegiance against their will. And in *Wooley v. Maynard*,[101] the Supreme Court had struck down a New Hampshire law requiring motorists to display the phrase "Live Free or Die" on their license plates. Requiring a motorist to display a license-plate message that was repugnant to him violated his First Amendment rights, the Supreme Court ruled, "because it 'forces an individual, as part of his daily life, indeed constantly while his automobile is in public view, to be an instrument for fostering adherence to an ideological point of view he finds unacceptable."[102]

In the Ninth Circuit's view, requiring students to display a motto on their school-uniform shirts "is not meaningfully distinguishable from the State of New Hampshire's inclusion of the motto 'Live Free or Die' on its license plates."[103] Nor did it matter, the court instructed, that students had ways to disclaim the school motto. Finally, the Ninth Circuit rejected the school district's argument that the motto "Tomorrow's Leaders" passed constitutional scrutiny because its message was innocuous and nonideological.

"Whether the First Amendment to the Constitution will permit officials to order observance of ritual of this nature does not depend upon whether as a voluntary exercise we would think it to be good, bad or merely innocuous. The Supreme Court's case law suggests that ideological speech is not the only form of forbidden compelled speech.[104]

The Ninth Circuit also ruled that the school's policy of exempting students from wearing the prescribed school uniform if they were wearing the uniform of a "nationally recognized" youth organization indicated a "content-specific distinction" that favored "certain clothing-related speech" (specifically the uniforms of the Boy Scouts and Girl Scouts) over other speech conveyed by clothing.

In short, the school's student-uniform policy was constitutionally suspect on two grounds. First, the school's motto on the uniforms' shirts constituted compelled speech. Second, the school's exemption for students wearing uniforms of nationally approved organizations was not content-neutral. These two infirmities required the case to be remanded back to a federal trial court for a "strict scrutiny review."[105] Specifically, the trial court was instructed to determine whether the inclusion of the "Tomorrow's Leaders" motto on student uniforms was "narrowly tailored to serve a compelling state interest."[106] In addition, the lower court was directed to determine whether the school's content-based exemption for students wearing alternative approved uniforms could survive strict scrutiny.

Frudden is an important case because it breaks an unbroken streak of wins for school districts when parents have challenged student-uniform policies on First Amendment grounds. The Ninth Circuit's conclusion that a Nevada school's tepid motto, "Tomorrow's Leaders," constitutes compelled speech when affixed to a student's school uniform raises the possibility that school mottos and emblems might be struck down in other contexts. Under the *Frudden* court's analysis, school mottos might be constitutionally suspect if they appeared on student identification cards; and a school mascot might also be challenged as compelled speech if it conveyed some sort of symbolic message and appeared on a football helmet or a cheerleader's uniform.

Moreover, the court's ruling that the student-uniform policy's exemption, which allowed students to come to school wearing the approved uniform of a nationally recognized youth organization, will prompt many school districts to review their school-uniform exemption policies to determine whether they would pass muster under the strict-scrutiny analysis that the Ninth Circuit ruled was the appropriate standard for determining an exemption's constitutionality.

Perhaps most disturbingly, at least from the perspective of school administrators, even the most innocuous and nonideological motto or emblem on a school uniform is subject to a First Amendment challenge under the Ninth Circuit's rationale in *Frudden*. The fact that a school's motto conveys no social or political message and is merely hortatory would not insulate it from a First Amendment challenge.

The final chapter of the *Frudden* saga has not yet been written. At the time of this writing, the lower court has yet to determine whether the Roy Gomm Elementary School policy can withstand strict scrutiny. If the lower court strikes the policy down, then it seems likely that the *Frudden* case will trigger a new round of legal challenges against school-uniform policies. If a school's policy calls for student uniforms to convey a message or contains an exemption allowing students to wear certain approved alternative types of clothing, then the policy may very well be invalidated by a federal court under principles laid down by the Ninth Circuit in *Frudden v. Pilling.*

CONCLUSION

In summary, two school-uniform cases were decided by state courts and seven were decided in the federal courts. The plaintiffs challenged school districts' student-uniform policies on a variety of grounds, including free speech, equal protection, due process, and the argument that mandatory school uniforms interfere with parents' constitutional right to direct the upbringing of their children. In eight of the nine cases, the school district prevailed and the school-uniform policy was deemed constitutional. The lone exception is the *Frudden* case discussed above, decided in 2014.

A comparison between dress-code litigation and school-uniform litigation reveals a stark difference in the way courts perceive the constitutionality of school-uniform policies as opposed to student dress codes. As illustrated in our previous volume, dress codes have a spotty record of survival when challenged in the courts, while school uniforms have a near perfect record of constitutional survival. Litigation involving dress codes tends to look more like potpourri than an articulated and unified body of litigation. The more restrictive policies of mandated school uniforms fared better in the courts than school districts' student dress codes.

In addition to the near perfect win/loss record for school uniforms, it is worth noting that the courts relied on different bodies of law when they reviewed challenges to school-uniform policies than when they reviewed school dress codes. In the student dress-code cases, courts relied primarily on *Tinker* to ascertain if student speech can be sanctioned for causing or reasonably forecasting a disruption in the school environment. *Bethel*, *Hazelwood*, and *Morse* were also cited, although much less frequently than *Tinker*. However, in student-uniform litigation, the courts have relied heavily on Supreme Court decisions that did not relate to schools or education, the *O'Brien* decision in particular.

In the future, school districts defending their student dress codes may find they are more successful if they describe their dress codes as content-neutral policies similar to student-uniform policies that have been upheld by the courts. *Palmer v. Waxahachie Independent School District*, involving a constitutional challenge to a very restrictive student dress code, may be indicative of the future.[107] In that case, the Fifth Circuit upheld a Texas school district's student dress code against a constitutional challenging, concluding that the district's student-dress policy was content neutral, that it furthered an important governmental interest, and that it had not been adopted to suppress unwanted student expression. The court also found that students had ample alternative forms of expression both within and outside the school day. In short, the Fifth Circuit analyzed the Waxahachie Independent School District's student-dress policy almost exactly as it had analyzed student uniforms in the *Canady* case and the *Forney* case.

In sum, school-uniform cases have not been decided by the courts on the basis of the Supreme Court's four seminal student free-speech cases: *Tinker*, *Fraser*, *Hazelwood*, and *Morse*. Instead, the courts have used the noneducation Supreme Court cases of *O'Brien*, *Spence*, and *Johnson.* They have looked to *O'Brien* to determine whether a school district's student-uniform policy passes intermediate scrutiny for content-neutral policies. Every time these three cases have been used to determine the constitutionality of a school-uniform policy, the policy has been upheld as constitutional. *Frudden*, the only federal court decision that did not rely on *O'Brien*, *Spence*, or *Johnson* to reach its decision, ruled against a school district's student-uniform policy on the novel basis that the school's uniforms constituted compelled speech and that the school's exemption for students wearing other uniforms approved by national youth organizations was not content-neutral.

It is highly likely that *O'Brien*, *Spence*, and *Johnson* will continue to influence student free-speech litigation associated with student attire, particularly in cases involving student uniforms. As we discussed in *Student Dress Codes and the First Amendment: Legal Challenges and Policy Issues*, we may also see a greater use of these constitutional tests in student dress-code cases.[108]

With *Frudden*, we see the interjection of two Supreme Court cases that were not used in other school-uniform cases; one arising in public education (*West Virginia Board of Education v. Barnette*) and the other involving adult free speech (*Wooley v. Maynard*). It seems possible that *Frudden* will have little impact on schools because they will avoid the issue of compelled speech by simply removing mottos and slogans from student uniforms. However, compelled-speech issues may surface in other venues. In particular, schools may find their school mascots and logos challenged on the ground that they compel unwilling students to express sentiments with which they disagree.

So far, courts have been inclined to accept school districts' arguments that they have a compelling interest in adopting school-uniform policies, in spite of the fact that educators have little evidence to support that assertion. As research accumulates on the impact of school uniforms, that research may be introduced to support the argument that school uniforms do not have a significant impact on academic achievement or student discipline. Researchers Brunsma and Rockquemore have compared school-uniform policies to "cleaning and brightly painting a deteriorating building in that on the one hand, it grabs our immediate attention; on the other hand, it is only a coat of paint."[109]

As of this writing, school uniforms have consistently passed constitutional muster, with only the *Frudden* case giving hope to school-uniform opponents. But school authorities should not confuse success in the courts with the success of student-uniform policies themselves. Is a mere change of clothes the answer, or part of the answer, to school reform; or, at the end of the school day, is it just a change of clothes? Our next chapter will explore the research on school uniforms.

NOTES

1. Todd A. DeMitchell and Mark A. Paige, "School Uniforms in the Public Schools: Symbol or Substance? A Law & Policy Analysis," *Education Law Reporter* 250 (2010): 847, 879.

2. A policy is a set of values issued with authority and expressed in written form or words. It is authoritative when there is sufficient power to induce a shift in behavior toward achieving specified values. See Catherine Marshall, Douglas Mitchell, and Frederick Wirt, *Culture and Education Policy in the American States* (New York: Falmer Press, 1989).

3. John W. Kingdon, *Agendas, Alternatives, and Public Policies*, 2nd ed. (New York: Longman, 2010).

4. United States Department of Education, *Manual on School Uniforms* (1996), http://www.ed.gov/updates/uniforms.html, p. 1.

5. William Jefferson Clinton, *Remarks by the President on School Uniform Program*, Jackie Robinson Academy, Long Beach California, February 24, 1996, available at http://www.ed.gov/pressreleases/02-1996/whpr28 and US Department of Education, *Manual on School Uniforms*, 1996, http://www.ed.gov/updates/uniforms.html.

6. Troy Y. Nelson, "If Clothes Make the Person, Do Uniforms Make the Student? Constitutional Free Speech Rights and Student Uniforms," *Education Law Reporter* 118 (1997): 1. (School uniforms can support a safe school if part of an overall safety program.)

7. The National Center for Education Statistics reported that school districts in high-poverty communities are far more likely to require students to wear school uniforms than districts in low-poverty communities. http://nces.ed.gov/programs/digest/d13/tables/dt13_233.50.asp.

8. E-mail correspondence May 28, 2009. Copies available from the authors.

9. Kate Zernicke, "Plaid's Out Again, as Schools Give Up Requiring Uniforms," *New York Times*, September 13, 2002, http://www.nytimes.com/2002/09/13/us/plaid-s-out-again-as-schools-give-up-requiring-uniforms.html.

10. Jennifer Steinhauer, "Bloomberg, With Promises to Keep, Says He Kept Many," *New York Times*, February 11, 2003, http://www.nytimes.com/2003/02/11/nyregion/bloomberg-with-promises-to-keep-says-he-kept-many.html.

11. Spence v. Washington, 418 U.S. 405, 410-411 (1974).

12. Isaacs v. Board of Education of Howard County, 40 F. Supp. 2d 335 (D.Md. 1999). See also Brandt v. Board of Education of City of Chicago, 480 F.3d 460, 465 (7th Cir. 2007), *cert. denied*, 128 S. Ct 441 (2007) (involving middle-school students who designed a T-shirt for school).

13. Fowler v. Williamson, 448 F. Supp. 497 (W.D.N.C. 1978).

14. 319 U.S. 624 (1943).

15. 526 F.3d 419, 428 (9th Cir. 2008).

16. 508 F. Supp. 2d 713 (E.D. Ark. 2007), *aff'd* 540 F.3d 752 (8th Cir. 2008), *cert. denied*, 129 S. Ct. 1526 (2009).

17. The school policy also stated that "No towel, scarf, bandana, do-rag, shirt, string, chain, jewelry, special button, insignia, label, marking, different-colored stitching, fringe, brad, stud, picture, logo, ribbon, embroidery, initials, monogram, special buckle, or any other form of adornment may be worn on or over any part of the uniform, except the school name, school logo, or school insignia." Lowry v. Watson Chapel School District, 540 F.3d 752, 756 n. 6 (8th Cir. 2008).

18. Ibid., 762.

19. Ibid., 766.

20. DePinto v. Bayonne Board of Education, 514 F. Supp. 2d 633, 636 (D. N.J. 2007).

21. Ibid., 644.

22. Ibid., 650.

23. Frudden v. Pilling, 742 F.3d 1199 (9th Cir. 2014).

24. Phoenix Elementary School District No. 1 v. Green, 943 P.2d 836 (Ariz. Ct. App. 1997).

25. 473 U.S. 788 (1985).

26. Ibid., 798.

27. Phoenix Elementary School District No. 1 v. Green, 943 P.2d at 839, quoting Hazelwood School District v. Kuhlmeier, 484 U.S. 260, 273 (1988).

28. Ibid.

29. *First Amendment Schools*. "What are the constitutional objections to mandatory dress codes and uniform policies? Association of Supervision and Curriculum Development (April 2015) available at www.firstamendmentschools.org/freedoms/faq.aspx?id=13001; Richard Riley, Manual on School Uniforms, U.S. Department of Education (September 1996) available at www2.ed.gov/offices/OSDFS/actguid/uniforms.html; California Education Code § 35183(7)(e).

30. Jennifer Starr, "School Violence and Its Effect on the Constitutionality of Public School Uniform Policies," *Journal of Law & Education* 29, no. 1 (2000): 113–18.

31. Byars v. City of Waterbury, 47 Conn. Supp. 342 (Conn. Super 2001).

32. Ibid., 361.

33. Ibid., 362.

34. Ibid., 364.

35. Ibid., 363.

36. The court did not require that the goals be met through a demonstration of statistically significant improvement. Ibid., 365.

37. Ibid.

38. Hicks v. Halifax County Board of Education, 93 F. Supp. 2d 649, 653-54 (E.D. N.C. 1999). The superintendent involved the communities of all nine elementary schools that would be affected by the school-uniform policy in a public discussion of the pros and cons of adopting the policy. The superintendent cited five benefits that accrue from wearing school uniforms: (1) improved student behavior, (2) increased safety in schools, (3) increased sense of belonging to the school, (4) increased emphasis on individual personality and achievement rather than outward appearance, and (5) elimination of distinctions between wealthy and needy children. Ibid., 652.

39. Ibid., 653.

40. Ibid., 657. For a discussion of the limits of the parental right to direct the upbringing of their child, see Todd A. DeMitchell and Joseph J. Onosko, "A Parent's Child and the State's Future Citizen: Judicial and Legislative Responses to the Tension over the Right to Direct and Education," *Southern California Interdisciplinary Law Journal* 22, no. 3 (2013): 591. The authors write:

> Courts have consistently placed the educational rights of parents beneath the rights of communities to create public schools deemed beneficial for the general welfare. Public schools must be allowed to reasonably pursue the educational goals of the community as established through the democratic process of electing school board members unencumbered by particular desires parents may have for their children.

Ibid., 634–35.

41. See Chalifoux v. New Caney Independent School District, 976 F. Supp. 659 (S.D. Tex. 1997) in which the federal district court used a hybrid test to review the constitutionality of a dress-code regulation against wearing rosaries, which school authorities considered to be gang apparel. Using strict-scrutiny analysis, the court found that the ban on rosaries was not the least restrictive means of controlling gang activity and making schools safe. The dress code placed an undue burden on the free exercise rights of students.

42. American Civil Liberties Union, News Release, "Student Prevails in NC School Uniform Dispute," January 11, 2000, https://www.aclu.org/free-speech/student-prevails-nc-school-uniform-dispute.

43. Vines v. Board of Education of Zion School District No. 6, 2002 WL 58815 (N.D. Ill. January 14, 2002).

44. Ibid., *3 citing Hazelwood School District v. Kuhlmeier, 484 U.S. 260, 273 (1988).

45. Ibid., *4.

46. Ibid. *4.

47. 240 F.3d 437 (5th Cir. 2001).

48. 491 U.S. 397 (1989).

49. 460 F.2d 609 (5th Cir. 1972).

50. Canady v. Bossier Parish School District, 240 F.3d at 439–40. See also Richards v. Thurston, 424 F.2d 1281, 1285 (1st Cir. 1970), in which the court stated that "a school rule that forbids skirts shorter than a certain length while on school grounds would require less justification than one requiring hair to be cut, which affects the student twenty-four hours a day, seven days a week, nine months a year." For a similar argument, see Isaacs v. Board of Education of Howard County, Maryland, 40 F. Supp. 2d 335, 339 (D. Md. 1999), which distinguished hairstyle regulations from dress-code regulations. "Headgear, like other clothing and unlike hair, is easily removed and replaced. Shermia is free to wear her headwrap outside of school and, apparently, is even free to wear the headwrap to and from school. The school rules simply require that she leave the headwrap in her locker during the school day."

51. Ibid., 440.

52. Ibid., 441.

53. Ibid.

54. Ibid.

55. Ibid., 441n3. "Our analysis simply acknowledges that certain choices of clothing may have sufficient communicative content to qualify as First Amendment activity." Ibid. However, the court expressly declined to define the contours of the "extent or type of clothing necessary to communicate a discrete message in order to afford First Amendment protection." Ibid.

56. Ibid.

57. Ibid., 443.

58. 121 F. Supp. 2d 621 (W.D. Ky. 2000).

59. Ibid., 627.

60. Littlefield v. Forney Independent School District, 268 F.3d 275, 283–284 n.8 (5th Cir. 2001). ("Regarding the 'coerced speech' argument, the students argue that mandatory uniforms convey a particularized message that the school district wishes to express, namely that students have respect for the authority of teachers and administrators, have Forney school and civic pride, and support school policies.")

61. Ibid., 284.

62. Ibid., 285.

63. Ibid., 286.

64. Ibid., 287.

65. Lowry v. Watson Chapel School District 508 F. Supp. 2d 713, 715 (E.D. Ark. 2007).

66. Ibid., 716.

67. 401 F.3d 381 (6th Cir. 2005).

68. 268 F.3d 275 (5th Cir. 2001).

69. Lowry v. Watson Chapel School District, 508 F. Supp. 2d at 719.

70. Ibid., 720 citing Canady v. Bossier Parish School District., 240 F.3d 437, 443 (5th Cir. 2001).

71. Ibid.

72. Derry v. Marion Community Schools, 790 F. Supp. 839, 842 (N.D. Ind. 2008).

73. The policy restricts hoodies, denim clothing, clothing with altered openings, bandanas, buttons, and attire signifying gangs. Ibid., 845.

74. Ibid., 846. The research was cited in the court case.

75. Ibid., 850.

76. Ibid.

77. Jacobs v. Clark County School District, 526 F.3d at 422.

78. Ibid. Interestingly, Kimberly Jacobs's grades improved during her suspensions.

79. Ibid., 427 ("prohibit[s] students from displaying any printed messages on their clothing, save for, in some cases, the school logo").

80. Ibid., 428 (school-uniform policy restricts students' ability to "express [their] individuality through forced uniformity").

81. Ibid. (plaintiffs "being forced to convey a message of uniformity . . . by wearing the same clothing as . . . classmates").

82. Ibid., 432.

83. Ibid., 433.

84. Ibid., 432.

85. Ibid., 433.

86. *United States v. O'Brien*, 391 U.S. at 376–77 (1968).

87. Jacobs v. Clark County School District, 526 F.3d at 435. ("Indeed, it is hard to think of a government interest more important than the interest in fostering conducive learning environments for our nation's children." Ibid., 435–36.).

88. Ibid., 436.

89. Ibid.

90. Ibid., 438.

91. Ibid., 441. Judge Thomas dissented, arguing that the case should have been analyzed under *Tinker*. Ibid., 443.

92. Frudden v. Pilling, 742 F.3d 1199, 1201 (9th Cir. 2014).

93. 842 F. Supp. 2d 1265 (D.Nev. 2012).

94. Riley v. National Federation of the Blind, Inc., 487 U.S. 781, 797 (1988).

95. Abood v. Detroit Board of Education, 431 U.S. 209, 234–35 (1977).

96. The Fruddens' alleged violations of their First Amendment expressive rights, First Amendment associational rights, procedural and substantive due process, equal protection, and viewpoint discrimination. Frudden, 742 F.3d at 1273–78.

97. The district court stated that the motto was "one team, one community." Frudden v. Pilling, 842 F. Supp. 2d 1265, 1274 (D.Nev. 2012). The Ninth Circuit Court of Appeals stated that the logo was "Tomorrow's Leaders." Frudden, 742 F.3d at 1201. No explanation for the difference in logos was offered by the appellate court. An internet search showed the use of the "Tomorrow's Leaders" logo.

98. Frudden, 842 F. Supp. 2d at 1274.

99. Frudden v. Pilling, 742 F.3d 1199, 1202–1203 (9th Cir. 2014) quoting Wooley v. Maynard, 430 U.S. 705, 714 (1977).

100. 319 U.S. 624 (1943).

101. 430 U.S. 705 (1977).

102. Frudden v. Pilling, 742 F.3d at 1203, citing Maynard v. Woolsey, 430 U.S at 715.

103. Ibid., 1205.

104. Ibid.,1206 (internal quotation marks and internal citation omitted).

105. Ibid., 1208.

106. Ibid., 1207.

107. 579 F.3d 502 (5th Cir. 2009).

108. Richard Fossey and Todd A. DeMitchell, *Student Dress Codes and the First Amendment: Legal Challenges and Policy Issues* (Lanham, MD: Rowman & Littlefield, 2014). See also Richard Fossey, Todd A. DeMitchell, and Suzanne Eckes, "The End of the T-Shirt Wars in the Public Schools? *Palmer v. Waxahachie Independent School District*," *Teachers College Record*, September 28, 2009, http://www.tcrecord.org ID Number: 15775.

109. David L. Brunsma and Kerry A. Rockquemore, "Effects of Student Uniforms on Attendance, Behavior Problems, Substance Use, and Academic Achievement," *Journal of Educational Research* 92, no. 1 (1998): 53, 60.

Chapter Five

Research on School Uniforms

Mixed Results

> So far, research on the effects of dress codes and school uniform policies is inconclusive and mixed. No clear trends have emerged. —Education Commission of the States[1]

The *Portsmouth Herald* (Portsmouth, New Hampshire) ran an op-ed on September 8, 2012 entitled "Dress Codes Help Schools Educate Our Children."[2] The editors, while not explicitly embracing school uniforms, wrote, "This is not a call for uniforms in public schools, but the positives of what a uniform dress provides can be effectively reached by reeling in the extremes."[3] What are the positives that the editorial references, and how do we know they exist as a result of students wearing a uniform to school?

The Fifth Circuit, in *Canady v. Bossier Parish School Board*, stated, "The School Board's purpose for enacting the uniform policy is to increase test scores and reduce disciplinary problems."[4] The Louisiana school district is not alone in adopting a mandatory school-uniform policy as a means to achieve, among other reasons, higher cognitive outcomes for its students and better behavior. If these are the rationales for the policy, do the policies yield positive results? In other words, if the hypothesis is that restrictions on student clothing choices will result in specified outcomes, does the research support the hypothesis?

Student behavioral change, school cultural change, and higher achievement, all for little to no cost, [school uniforms] must be the holy grail of school remedies.

Source: Todd A. DeMitchell, "School Uniforms: There Is No Free Lunch," *Teachers College Record*, December 14, 2006, available at http://www.tcrecord.org, ID Number 12891.

Many schools contemplating the adoption of a mandatory school-uniform policy turn to research to assist in the decision to adopt and what process to use to adopt. For example, Valley View Elementary School in Columbia Heights, Minnesota announced that starting in the fall of 2013 students would be wearing blue and yellow school uniforms. The school asserted that uniforms "provide a sense of unity and school identity," "instill pride," and "allow students to focus on their attention on learning."[5] The school supported these conclusions by citing research by M. Sue Stanley discussed below. This is standard practice, but it is interesting to note the venue in which the school district cited school-uniform research. Valley View Elementary School was seeking $5,000 for its school-uniform kick-off using the fundraising site Razoo to solicit donations for the program. The research was prominently placed as part of its online solicitation.

Changing schools and changing student attitudes and work habits involve heavy lifting. Developing a constitutionally sound school-uniform policy is part of the heavy lifting but it is important to adopt a policy that actually delivers what it promises: a policy that promotes improved student achievement and that establishes a school environment that leads to better academic outcomes. As asserted in *Jacobs v. Clark County School* District,[6] wearing a school uniform promotes safety, focuses on achievement, eliminates visible differences in wealth, and makes it easier for families to manage their clothing budgets. But does a school uniform really promote those goals? Or does a school uniform offer the illusion of school reform without requiring more substantive changes in school policy?

We will briefly review research on school uniforms in order to provide a foundation for our readers to assist them in understanding the fundamental assertion of school-uniform proponents. Data-driven decision-making requires an understanding of the existing research. Research may well not be the final arbiter of the decision to adopt a school-uniform policy, but it is essential for school leaders to know what the research says about benefits of school uniforms before making a decision to adopt such a policy for their school district.

SETTING THE RESEARCH STAGE

We focus on school-uniform research because proponents of school uniforms assert that requiring students to wear school uniforms results in certain positive student academic outcomes and behaviors. Supporters of school-uniform policies believe that uniforms curb negative behaviors and reinforce positive behaviors. However, proponents of dress codes, which generally offer students more choices about the clothing they wear than school-uniform policies, typically do not base their policy on student outcomes. Instead, they typically state that some types of student attire are unacceptable (e.g., tube tops, halter tops, cut-off shorts, sleepwear, and clothes promoting alcohol or drugs). The dress code seeks to clarify and enforce standards of acceptable conduct related to clothing choices. The underlying assumption is not that a prohibition of wearing a T-shirt advertising drugs or alcohol translates into better student achievement, better attendance, and a sense of school community. Such a prohibition does, however, remove distractions from the school environment.

When school leaders develop, implement, and enforce student dress codes, they generally do so to achieve a particular behavioral or academic outcome. They simply believe that certain types of clothing are unacceptable for our schools. Not allowing students to wear advertisements for drugs, lewd T-shirts, or to display underwear is important because those clothing choices diminished the culture of the school. Stopping a student from wearing unacceptable clothing is the goal and the measure of success. Increased test scores, esprit de corps in the school, and better attendance are generally not the purposes of a student dress code.

Consequently, research on the impact of dress codes on student academic and behavioral outcomes is hard to find. Indeed, the Fifth Circuit of Appeals held that a Texas school district was not required to show statistical evidence to support its claims that its student dress code improved the school environment. The court wrote, "We do not, however, require statistical or scientific evidence to uphold a dress code; improvements in discipline or morale cannot always be quantified."[7]

School-uniform policies, however, are generally adopted for the expressed purpose of promoting tangible changes in school culture and student achievement, and quite a bit of research has been conducted to determine if school uniforms actually deliver the benefits their proponents often promise. We will begin our exploration of the research on school uniforms with a discussion of an early study that we conducted with our colleague Casey Cobb from the University of Connecticut.

THE RESEARCH

In the last decade, according to the National Center for Education Statistics (NCES), the number of school districts that had adopted student dress codes remained relatively constant, with just under 50 percent of the reporting school districts enforcing a strict dress code. There was bump up in the 2007–2008 report for both elementary and secondary schools, but the following three-year report (2011–2012) showed a very slight decline from the numbers reported in the 2003–2004 report. More secondary schools than elementary schools enforced a dress code. Thus, dress codes appear to be part of the policy infrastructure of many public schools. However, while the number of school districts that have formal student dress codes showed little fluctuation between the years 2003 and 2012, federal data shows that the number of school districts that have adopted school-uniform policies went up significantly (see Figure 5.1).

Principals, Dress Codes, and School Uniforms: A Matter of Perception

Our study, *Dress Codes in the Public Schools: Principals, Policies, and Precepts*,[8] published with Casey Cobb in 2000, focused on the perceptions of school principals who are tasked with enforcing dress codes and school-uniform policies. The study reported on the perceptions of 157 principals drawn from a national sample. The survey instrument asked six Likert-type questions[9] and one open-ended question: “In your own words, succinctly state why a dress code policy is needed or not in your school.” In addition, we analyzed the dress codes that were sent to us. We will first discuss the data on dress codes and then conclude with the data on the perceptions of the responding principals with regard to school uniforms.

The Likert-type scale was a five-point scale with anchors of one = strongly disagree and five = strongly agree. The responses were aggregated and disaggregated for school level (elementary, middle, and high school) and by

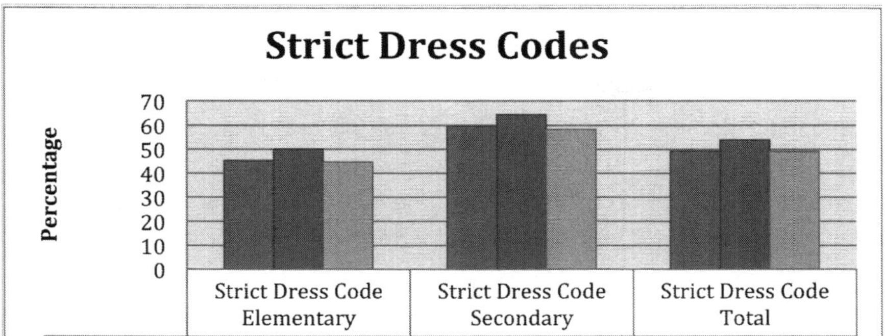

	Strict Dress Code Elementary	Strict Dress Code Secondary	Strict Dress Code Total
2003-2004	45.2	59.7	49.3
2007-2008	50	64.4	54
2011-2012	44.6	58.3	49.1

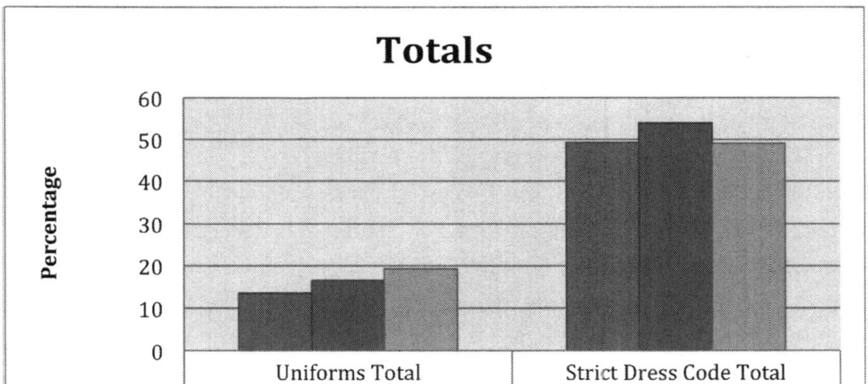

	Uniforms Total	Strict Dress Code Total
2003-2004	13.5	49.3
2007-2008	16.5	54
2011-2012	19.3	49.1

Figure 5.1. Digest of Education Statistics (Table 233.50, Percentage of public and private schools with various safety and security measures, by school level: 2003–04, 2007–08, and 2011–12). *National Center for Education Statistics* http://nces.ed.gov/programs/digest/d13/tables/dt13_233.50.asp

location (rural, suburban, and urban). Eighty principals had dress codes and sixty-four did not.

There was support from the responding principals for dress codes (range 3.40 to 4.00). All of the means for dress codes were above the midpoint (3) of the scale. The highest mean (4.00) was question #4, "I believe that dress codes are worth the trouble of enforcing." The lowest mean (3.40) was question #2, "Students do not have a constitutional right to wear clothes of their choice to school." According to the study's findings, most principals believe that students have a constitutional right to wear the clothes of their choice to school, but their view is not strong. Therefore, it can be asserted that there is a constitutional area where some restrictions on student attire choices do not offend constitutional protection. When the questions on the impact of dress codes on student behavior (#1), realities of the work world (#3), worth of enforcing (#4), and reduction of sexual harassment (#5) were collapsed into a subset, the mean is 3.86. While high-school principals showed a larger degree of support for dress codes than elementary- and middle-school principals, the difference was not significant. Principals in rural areas showed greater support for the dress code subset than principals in suburban and urban schools. There was no significant difference between locations.

However, it is interesting to note that none of the means was above 4.0 (showing agreement). While there was support for dress codes, the support was solid but not overwhelming. The only disaggregated scores that were above 4.0 were from high-school principals.

The review of submitted dress codes categorized the code provisions into three categories: Provisions that Occurred Most Frequently, Provisions that Occurred With Some Frequency, and Provisions that Rarely Occurred.[10] The Occurring Most Frequently sections included prohibited categories such as halters, low-cut tops, sagging pants (pants must be "worn at the natural waistline"), hairnets, do-rags, and sunglasses inside school buildings. Length of skirts and shorts, bare midriffs, and lots of references to shoes were found in the codes. It is most likely that courts would not find that these choices in clothing would carry sufficient expressive content as to warrant free speech protection under the First Amendment. A second most frequently occurring category is banned communications—messages about drugs, alcohol, or tobacco, and lewd, vulgar, and offensive statements, including sexually related or suggestive comments (these could most likely be considered as contrary to the school's mission). The last category addressed the issue of clothing that is disruptive, such as gang attire.[11]

The second category of Occurring with Some Frequency is organized into two parts: mandates and prohibitions. The mandates are straightforward and are what one would expect in any setting in which individuals come together in a work-type setting. They include:

- Hair must be clean and well groomed.
- Clothes must be clean and neat.
- Clothes must be fastened, or buttoned properly and there must be no dangling belts.[12]

The prohibitions include, naming a few:

- No spandex or bicycle shorts
- No torn, frayed, ripped clothing, or clothing with holes in it
- No body piercing
- No derogatory, intimidating, threatening, mocking, or ridiculing statements
- No clothing that might "cause undue attention to an individual student"
- No statements supportive of cults or Satan
- No statements that promote violence[13]

As we discussed in chapter 2, several of these prohibitions run the risk of being vague and thus violative of Fourteenth Amendment substantive due-process requirements.

The last category is a hodge-podge of provisions that only occurred once or twice in the dress codes we reviewed. They include such items as no black lipstick, no hair rollers, and no swimming attire. Of note, however, are two prohibitions that could receive scrutiny in the second decade of the twenty-first century: no cross-dressing and no visible tattoos.

Turning to the principals' perception of school uniforms, our study found only mixed support. The mean for question #6, "I support the implementation of a mandatory school uniform policy," was the lowest in the study, 3.13. As stated above, high-school principals had greater support—although not statistically significant—for dress codes than middle-school and elementary-school principals. But when asked their level of support for uniforms, high-school principals did not support uniforms ($M = 2.82$). They differed significantly from middle- ($M = 3.50$) and elementary-school principals ($M = 3.12$) who supported school uniforms. A Tukey post hoc analysis indicated that high-school principals scored significantly lower than middle-school principals.[14] Urban principals ($M = 3.42$) showed greater support for uniforms followed by suburban ($M = 3.13$) and then rural principals ($M = 3.02$).[15] Interestingly, the level of support is exactly opposite for dress codes. Whereas school-uniform support differed by location with urban, suburban, and rural in descending order of support, support for dress codes descends from high to low with rural principals indicating the most support followed by suburban principals, and urban principals indicating the lowest level of support. The authors were not able to identify any reason for the switch in support by location.

The last part of the study asked why a dress code was needed or not needed at their school. In total, 85 percent supported dress codes. Two-thirds of responding elementary-school principals stated support for a dress code. As an example of support, one principal simply wrote, "Sloppy clothes can enhance sloppy behavior." And an elementary-school principal wrote, begging the question of the application of dress codes and school uniforms to educators, "I personally believe that teachers should have one first."[16]

Thirty-one of the thirty-two responding middle-school principals supported dress codes in this section of the study. The reasons given for supporting dress codes included: responding to gangs, curbing disruptions, and reducing peer pressure. While one principal wrote, "Proper Dress = Success," another wrote, "It eliminates the bizarre." The lone principal who believed that a dress code was not necessary stated, somewhat enigmatically, "Our culture has changed and this move wouldn't save it."[17]

For high-school principals, thirty-two of thirty-four responding principals gave their support to dress codes. They expressed the view that a dress code sets expectations and standards, reduces distractions, and reflects the work world students would soon be entering. One principal wrote that dress codes "make them look like students, help them to act like students."[18] However, one of the two dissenters wrote, "No need to stir the water."[19]

Overall, this study found principal support for dress codes. The support cut across level of school and location of school. It did not find the same level of support for school uniforms. In fact, it found that high-school principals did not support school uniforms.

Another principal-perception study was conducted around the same time as our study. The National Association of Elementary School Principals (NAESP), with support from Lands' End, a supplier of school uniforms, conducted a nationwide telephone survey of 755 principals; 90 percent were elementary-school principals. Seventy-one percent of the principals did not have a school-uniform policy and were not considering adopting such a policy. Twenty-nine percent of the principals who did not have a school-uniform policy stated that their dress code was sufficient. Of the remainder of the principals who had policies in their schools, ninety-five (12.6 percent of the 755) had a uniform policy in place for more than three years. These responding principals reported that school uniforms had a positive effect on the school's image in the community (84 percent), classroom discipline (79 percent), peer pressure (76 percent), school spirit (72 percent), concentration on schoolwork (67 percent), and student safety (62 percent).[20]

The principals with school-uniform policies supported their policies. However, less than 15 percent of the responding principals had school-uniform policies in their schools. In several of the following studies, the issue of educator perceptions of their existing policy was explored in which educators generally seemed supportive of their existing policies. A question that we explore below is whether the students share the same perception as their teachers and principals.

> I am a strong supporter of uniforms. I see a real difference in student demeanor, student behavior, and focus on work.
>
> Nancy Dickerson, Principal
> Mattahunt Elementary School
> Boston, Massachusetts
>
> Source: Lands' End, *School Uniforms: Why and How*, 2002, available at http://www.landsend.com/pdfs/how_why_survey.pdf?sid=CGI2K_SID&refer=SCHOOLSURVEY0603. This open letter to educators and parents discusses the National Association of Elementary School Principal study on principal perceptions of school uniforms. See *supra* note 18.

As seen by these two studies, principals are more likely to find that dress codes meet the needs for appropriate student attire than school uniforms. This does not mean that there is not support among principals for school uniforms but the DeMitchell, Fossey, and Cobb study found that high-school principals in their study tended not to support school uniforms. Similarly, the NAESP study, which was overly weighted toward elementary-school principals, does not provide a counterweight to the divide by school level regarding support for school uniforms. The lack of clear support by principals for mandatory school uniforms may be reflected in the policy positions of the two major principal associations, the National Association of Elementary School Principals and the National Association of Secondary School Principals. We searched but could not find a policy position statement for either professional principal organization advocating school uniforms or eschewing school uniforms as strategies to improve student behavior, academic outcomes, and school culture and community. In other words, neither organization has a formal policy position with regard to school uniforms.

Studies of School Uniforms

Public schools adopt school-uniform policies to a lesser degree than dress codes. In 2011–2012, the National Center for Education Statistics showed that 49 percent of public-school districts enforced dress codes but just over 19 percent implemented school-uniform policies. However, the number of schools requiring school uniforms has increased 43 percent from 2003–2004 to 2011–2012 (see Figure 5.2). With the rise in school-uniform policies, there is a need to understand the research on the claims made by uniform proponents so as to properly weigh whether a school-uniform policy is best for a specific school.

One of the earliest studies of the impact of school uniforms on student behavior is M. Sue Stanley's study of the Long Beach Unified School District. Uniform advocates have used this study to support their policy choice. Stanley found in a two-year study of district data that suspensions decreased in elementary school by 28 percent and middle school by 36 percent, assault

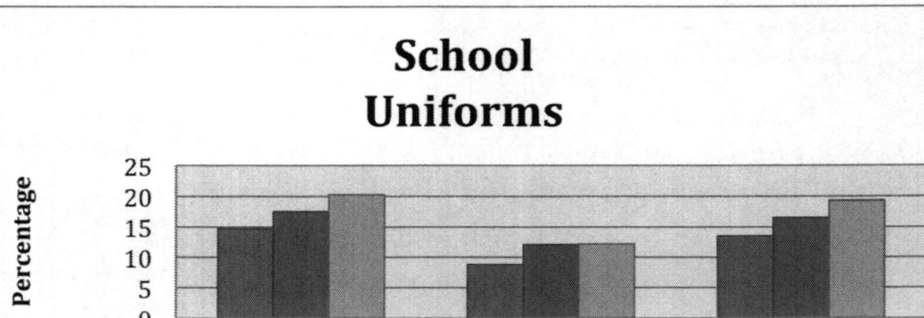

	Uniforms Elementary	Uniforms Secondary	Uniforms Total
2003-2004	14.7	8.8	13.5
2007-2008	17.5	12.1	16.5
2011-2012	20.3	12.2	19.3

Figure 5.2. Digest of Education Statistics (Table 233.50, Percentage of public and private schools with various safety and security measures, by school level: 2003–04, 2007–08, and 2011–12), ***National Center for Education Statistics*** **http://nces.ed.gov/programs/digest/d13/tables/dt13_233.50.asp**

and battery declined 34 percent, as did fighting (51 percent); and sex offenses decreased by 74 percent.[21]

In addition, elementary- and middle-school administrators perceived that uniforms had a positive influence on student behavior. They also perceived fewer class disruptions, increased work ethic, improved student attitude, and fewer playground fights. Teachers, counselors, and parents also reported positive perceptions regarding student interactions. In addition to perceptions, Stanley concluded that data on classroom disruptions, playground disruptions, and suspensions "clearly support the link between school uniforms and school safety."[22] These data support a finding that school uniforms resulted in behavioral changes in Long Beach students.

However, Stanley's findings indicated that middle-school students believed that uniforms did not reduce fights, help them to become part of the school, or help them to feel safer going to and from school. Similarly, elementary-school students stated that the school uniform did not make them fight less or feel a part of the school.[23]

Stanley offers the following explanation for the discrepancy in perceptions between adults and students about the value of school uniforms. Adult responses may reflect adult responses to wearing uniforms similar to Huss's discussion (below) of attribution theory to explain the perceptions of the teachers in his qualitative study. Second, Stanley suggested a novel explanation: that students were bored with the uniforms and that by the end of the year the uniforms may have been "too small, were discolored and faded, or just worn out."[24] Does this mean that a school can expect a diminishing return as the school year progresses and that wearing school uniforms will make students more restive toward the end of the school year?

However, Stanley urged caution in the use of her results. First, she acknowledged, the data may reflect the "Hawthorne effect" in which changes are the result of short-term visibility and attention associated with a new policy. Also, the decrease in crime that her study documented may have been the result of other policies and thus not entirely attributable to the uniform policy. She concludes, "Exciting as these results are, it is important to remember that they are *preliminary*, first-year results in a longitudinal study."[25]

Nonetheless, the results suggest that uniforms may have a positive impact on school safety. Because they are low-cost interventions that are unlikely to do harm, it appears they are worth considering.

Source: M. Sue Stanley, *supra* note 21, 434.

Brunsma and Rockquemore contributed to the research on school uniforms by conducting a large-scale study using the National Educational Longitudinal Study of 1988. They sought to determine whether school uniforms decreased substance abuse and behavioral problems, and whether they increased attendance and academic achievement.[26] They found that school uniforms did not have a direct effect on behavioral or academic outcomes of students. They concluded that adopting a school-uniform policy was largely a symbolic exercise.

On the other hand, Bodine disagreed with the findings of Brunsma and Rockquemore, citing methodological problems that formed the basis for their findings.[27] Other research studies have produced mixed results, with some finding no correlation between uniforms and academic achievement[28] while others found a relationship.[29] The research data are mixed as to whether school uniforms are an influential enough variable to improve academics, discipline, attendance, and self-esteem. Consequently, implementing school uniforms as a strategy to reduce violence, improve achievement, improve attendance, and build school spirit cannot be achieved with a strong sense that the data support the policy.

In addition to his research with Rockquemore, David L. Brunsma's *The School Uniform Movement and What It Tells Us about American Education: A Symbolic Crusade*[30] reviewed a number of studies on school uniforms. His literature review started with perception studies, including the two discussed above. Next Brunsma reviewed six small-scale studies. He concluded that these small-scale studies are not "useful as generalizable evidence that can be used by other schools struggling with the decision to implement a uniform policy."[31] The six studies reviewed drew conflicting conclusions as to the effectiveness of school uniforms.

For example, Carolyn Williams-Davidson's dissertation, a mixed-methodology study completed at Arizona State University in 1996, found no effects from school uniforms that could not be traced to other school procedures and policies.[32] Similarly, Mary Louise Murphy's dissertation, completed at the University of Washington in 1997, concluded that a rise in test scores and a drop in behavioral referrals experienced after an elementary-school student-uniform policy was implemented could be attributed to school uniforms being part of a larger comprehensive plan.[33]

A third doctoral dissertation out of Texas Southern University (1999) was reviewed by Brunsma. Henry L. Stevenson studied twenty-eight public Texas middle and high schools to determine whether school uniforms had any impact on discipline. He found no significant decreases in school discipline incidents, fights, weapons possession, assault/battery, or suspensions. However, he did find that improved attendance and a decrease in the number of expulsions were statistically significant.[34]

Brunsma concludes that there is overwhelming evidence that "uniform policies are not effective."[35] They have no significant impact on student perceptions of their safety, and no significant impact on achievement (kindergarten, first grade, elementary, eighth grade, or tenth grade). Furthermore, according to Brunsma school uniforms have no significant impact on eighth-grade and tenth-grade attendance, behavioral problems, or drug use, and no significant impact on kindergartners' self-control or coping skills. In fact, Brunsma asserts, "[u]niforms have solidly negative impact on aggregate achievement in high school."[36] He concludes school uniforms "have not been effective at attacking the very outcomes and issues they were assumed to aid:

1. reduction of violence and behavioral problems;
2. fostering school unity and improving the learning environment;
3. reducing social pressures and leveling status differentials;
4. increasing student self-esteem;
5. saving parents money on clothing for their children;
6. improving attendance; and ultimately
7. improving academic achievement."[37]

Another study that used large data sets is Ryan Yeung's 2009 study entitled "Are School Uniforms a Good Fit? Results from the ECLS-K and NELS."[38] This study utilized a large national data set very similar to Brunsma's study and reviewed data on public and private schools. Using the ECLKS-K data Yeung concluded, "Uniform effects appear to have little to no effect, and a negative effect, if any at all."[39] Using the NELS data, the analysis, using value-added scores rather than test-score levels, found that students in public schools with a school uniform policy score a third of a point higher in tenth-grade reading than children who are not required to wear uniforms; "on every other examination, public school students who are required to wear uniforms actually score worse than their counterparts who do not face the same restriction."[40] Yeung concludes from his analysis of two major national data sets that the results are remarkably consistent: "There is little evidence that uniforms improve achievement in schools."[41]

Not all research has reached the same conclusion as Brunsma and Yeung regarding the impact of school uniforms. However, their conclusions and the extent of their research are compelling and cannot be easily dismissed because the overall findings of this research do not support the current policy arguments in favor of school uniforms.

Seunghee Han used a large national data set similarly to the method used by Brunsma and Yeung. Han's research reviewed the School Survey on Crime and Safety 2003–2004 data set.[42] The study examined whether a mandatory school-uniform policy is associated with student problem behaviors. The study reviewed principals' reports of student behavior associated with firearms, drugs, physical attacks, gangs, and insubordination. Schools with mandatory school-uniform policies were compared with schools without such a policy.

A regression analysis found that elementary and middle schools with school uniforms had fewer student problem behaviors.[43] However, high schools with mandatory school uniforms had a greater frequency of student misbehavior.[44] Thus, the gains tended to disappear in high school. Interestingly, but not surprisingly, Han found that parental involvement at the elementary-school level has a significant ($p < .001$) impact on reducing the number of student negative behaviors.[45] At the high-school level, multiple teacher-training programs resulted in fewer problem student behaviors ($p < .001$). Han concluded that "school uniform policies might be considered to prevent or reduce students' problem behaviors."[46]

Another example of school-uniform research is John A. Huss's qualitative research on a K–5 school of 397 students in a city of twenty-four thousand.[47] Huss studied six teachers selected through a stratified purposive sample. The method employed case-study research with no hypothesis testing. He states the data captured the *initial* impressions of the respondents (emphasis is in original).[48]

Huss found that the teachers perceived an improvement in the school in two categories: socio/emotional aspects of school climate and cognitive aspects of school climate. He noted greater levels of respect, caring, and trust in the school after the implementation of the uniform policy based on teacher responses. For example, one teacher responded, "I think the students treat one another with more consideration and they are less apt to ridicule certain children because they are not wearing the 'right' [c]lothes."[49] The teachers reported better morale, school spirit, and enthusiasm for the school. All six teachers also perceived improvement in discipline at the school and fewer classroom disruptions and incidents of quarreling among students.[50]

The teachers perceived an improvement in academics and motivation. One teacher noticed an increased sense of responsibility and another reported greater participation in classroom activities and a more effective use of instructional time. A third teacher offered his opinion stating, "I think they focus more on their work. The kids get more time on task because there are fewer distractions."[51] Overall, the six teachers perceived that school uniforms enhanced the learning environment, enriched the quality of interactions between faculty and students, and improved discipline. All of these major changes resulted from one year of wearing school uniforms.

The only negative data point to the rosy portrait of the impact of school uniforms was the documentation on the number of discipline referrals that ticked up slightly from an average of 11.67 during the year preceding the implementation of the policy to 11.71 during the first year of school uniforms. Suspensions dropped from five to three yet referrals remained basically the same. Infractions for failing to comply with the uniform policy were not counted as part of the discipline referrals.[52] The teacher perceptions of fewer distractions and improved discipline may not be supported by the quantitative data.

Three teachers may have captured the position of why the number of discipline referrals remained stubbornly unchanged with the implementation of the school uniforms. They "revealed a clear preference toward school uniforms, and a subsequent indictment of students who did not [support school uniforms]."[53] The study did supply data on the numbers or percentages of students who did not comply with the school-uniform policy so as to provide a basis for comparison with those who did wear the uniform. The teachers stated:

- Ms. Barry: "The kinds [of students] wearing uniforms are less cocky toward adults."
- Mr. Clark: "It seems like the kids who perform at the lowest levels are the very kids who do not comply with the policy."

- Ms. Flanagan: "The students in my class who are responsible enough to wear their uniforms are more responsible in other ways, like homework, like paying attention, like studying for tests, the whole gamut."[54]

Is the implication that students would be better behaved and would learn more if only they wore school uniforms? These teachers' observations suggest that they believe that it is the uniform that makes the difference in student behavior, and that non-uniform-wearing students are the irresponsible ones. Huss suggests that through attribution, the school uniform "is a signifier of role identity that creates an expectation that the wearer has a particular character, whether the character is actually present or not."[55] Or, conversely, is there a *sub rosa* belief that the positive impact of school uniforms does not reach all students? Apparently, it is only those students who are already responsible for whom school uniforms work.

If this assumption is true, is wearing a school uniform transformative for the less responsible? A parent in a study of Bradford Middle School's school-uniform policy reflected this position, writing, "and, if your kid is good, it doesn't matter if they've [sic] got a red polo and a pair of khakis on or if they [sic] are wearing jeans and a t-shirt."[56] Implicit in these examples is the question: do school uniforms really make any difference with regard to school discipline and academic achievement?

Underscoring the mixed results found by Huss of teacher support for uniforms but counter evidence of no change in student behavior, we will briefly survey a few dissertations that arrived at differing conclusions. For example, Kathy S. Samuels's 2003 dissertation at the University of Alabama, Birmingham found that student achievement increased (1995–1998), discipline referrals decreased (1994–1999), and average daily attendance increased (1994–1998) after school uniforms were implemented.[57] Her research supports school uniforms as a positive school-reform strategy.

However, Pamela Y. Hoffler-Riddick's 1998 dissertation on school uniforms and attendance, grade point average, and self-esteem found less support for uniforms. Her study focused on ninth-grade students who had attended schools with uniforms for two consecutive years. Discipline referrals dipped significantly the first year that uniforms were mandated but rose significantly in the second year, raising the issue of whether the Hawthorne effect was present during the first year. She stated, "Data collected as part of this study do not support the notion that students who wear uniforms will come to school more, behave better, get better grades, or feel better about themselves."[58]

Wesley Scott Johnson's 2010 dissertation, completed at East Carolina University, studied the impact of school uniforms on safety.[59] He studied thirty-eight high schools, using data from North Carolina's Department of Public Instruction on incidents of school crime and violence and suspension and expulsions from 2004 to 2009. He found the following:

1. Thirty-one high schools (81.6 percent) experienced no sustained change in the incidents of crime and violence, while four (10.5 percent) showed a positive change, and three (7.9 percent) had a negative change.[60]
2. Thirty high schools (79.0 percent) experienced no change in the number of suspensions between pre- and post-school uniforms. Six (15.8 percent) had a positive change, and two (5.2 percent) experienced a negative change in numbers of suspension.[61]
3. Eighty percent of the responding assistant principals and principals agreed or strongly agreed that school uniforms help recognize outsiders, improve classroom behavior, restrict gang attire, and make the school environment safer.[62]
4. Sixty-one percent of the responding principals and assistant principals agreed or strongly agreed that school uniforms reduced referrals, suspensions, severe discipline incidents, and crime and violence.[63]

Johnson concluded, even though only a few schools reported positive changes as a result of implementing a school-uniform policy, the clear majority of the thirty-eight North Carolina high schools "produced no consistent or sustainable change" according to the data examined.[64] However, these data are not consistent with the perceptions of the school administrators. This inconsistency between data and perception or between perception of adults and students are also found in Hoffler-Riddick's 1998 dissertation, Stanley's study of Long Beach Unified School District, and Huss's research discussed above.

Wade and Stafford find the issue of perceptual differences of educators in their research.[65] Their study reviewed the perceptions of teachers (83) and students (415) in urban middle schools regarding the impact of school uniforms. They found that teachers perceived less gang violence whereas students perceived no change. In addition, their research indicated that students from schools that did not have school uniforms reported higher self-perception scores than students who attended schools with school uniforms. Once again, as noted above, there is a difference in perceptions between adults and students on the impact of school uniforms.

Elisabetta Gentile and Scott A. Imberman, from the University of Houston, conducted the last study we will review.[66] They studied the effects of a school-uniform policy on student achievement and behavior in a large urban school district in the Southwest. The students were disaggregated into two groups: grades 1–5 and grades 6–12. While the elementary grade configuration makes sense, the lumping of middle-school with high-school students does not account for the differences between the organizational levels and the developmental levels of middle and high schools. To treat the middle-school student and the high-school student as the same for research purposes presents methodological problems.

The researchers start with an interesting observation that has implications for understanding the potential outcomes school uniform research. They state in the introduction as well as in the conclusion that data may "suffer from substantial bias"[67] because the schools that adopt school uniforms may be responding to the existing behavior and achievement levels of their students and thus have selected uniforms as an appropriate response. With this caution stated, the researchers found the following in their analysis of the impact of school uniforms.

1. Discipline

    - There was no change in in-school and out-of-school suspensions for elementary-school students resulting from wearing school uniforms.
    - Among middle- and high-school students, there are statistically significant increases in in-school suspensions and reductions in out-of-school suspensions. The increases in in-school suspensions were greater than the reductions of out-of-school behavior. The researchers speculated that the increases in in-school suspensions "could be due to punishments for students who violate the uniform codes rather than a net increase in other behavioral incidents."[68] If this explanation is accepted, it means that school uniforms caused more disciplinary actions and thus required educators to expend resources responding to school-uniform infractions.

- The rate of infractions, while increasing in the initial years, declined in the years following the implementation of the uniform policy.
- Disciplinary infractions were increasing steadily prior to adoption in the middle and high schools and then appeared to level off, "suggesting that uniforms arrested the upward trend."[69]

2. Attendance

- "For elementary students there is little evidence of improvement in attendance. Girls show no significant change while boys show a statistically significant drop."[70]
- Attendance rates for girls in grades 6–12 increased to approximately one full day a year while boys increased by about one-half day.[71]

3. Academic Gains

- Wearing a school uniform resulted in little impact on test scores, although middle- and high-school scores were negative and "marginally significant." Using a second statistical model, the results for reading and math were confirmed with a slight improvement (not statistically significant at the .05 level).

This study provides weak to tepid support for school uniforms as a strategy to improve behavior, increase attendance, and show academic gains. The results are mixed, and where there is a reported statistically significant difference, it tended to be at the .10 level as opposed to the commonly accepted, and more rigorous, .05 level.

However, the researchers did find a novel outcome of wearing uniforms to school. "[W]e find that uniforms reduce the likelihood that girls leave the district for other schools."[72] Building on this finding, they conclude their report by suggesting that schools may use uniforms as a strategy "to prevent the loss of students to charters and other alternative education options."[73] They appear to have identified another positive outcome for mandating school uniforms; they are a retention strategy for schools that are losing female students to other schools.

CONCLUSION

Nine-year-old Olivia Ryan, clad in her New York City uniform, offered her opinion about wearing a uniform to school, stating, "I don't really think that they're going to act better because of what you're wearing. You're still the same person inside. You're just wearing something different."

Source: Sharmain Lewis and Monique Bishop, "The School Uniform Debate Continues," *New York Amsterdam News*, June 11, 1998.

The research on the impact of school uniforms on student behavior, discipline, connection to the school, attendance, and academic gains is at best mixed. Research findings are inconsistent not only with regard to the impact of school uniforms but also with regard as to whether the impact is positive or negative. If school uniforms are sold on the basis of the positive changes they will bring about, it seems reasonable to expect that research would support such claims. Unfortunately, from the perspective of school-uniform advocates, research findings that support the adoption of a school-uniform policy are sparse and conflicting.

The arguments for school uniforms ranged from capturing the benefits of equalizing the student attire field through "simplicity, practicality, and frugality"[74] to arguments that school uniforms will positively impact student behaviors, help positively identify students with their schools, and help bring about higher educational attainment.

It is true that students bonding with their schools has been found to have positive benefits. Students who form a positive affiliation or social bond are "less likely to engage in problem behaviors."[75] Businesses that sell school uniforms often tout the social benefits of bonding that supposedly results from students wearing uniforms. For example, Executive Apparel asserts in its website that young people find it difficult to take pride in their school because of "disjointed feelings among the student body."[76] The apparel company states that a school uniform helps to smooth out social, cultural, and financial differences among students that separate students. Wearing a school uniform levels these barriers, the company asserts, making "it more possible for young people to connect and support their school, because they feel more like a part of it."[77] The company cites no research for its conclusion and we find none to support the claim that school uniforms lead to school bonding for students.

No string of studies indicates that the stated positive outcomes from wearing school uniforms manifests in the changed behavior of students. It is the large-scale studies using national data sets that tend to find data that indicates that uniforms can actually have a negative impact on the school environment. However, the school- and school-district-level data point to a fairly consistent finding. Educators in schools where a school uniform has been mandated tend to ascribe positive outcomes to students wearing a school uniform.

However, several studies challenge the perceptions of educators by countervailing data on student behavior and show that educators' perceptions are often in opposition to those of their students. Educators are more positive about the impact of school uniforms while students are more skeptical about the impact of uniforms. Are adult educators more inclined than their students to find school-uniform policies beneficial because the policies were mandated by the adults?

Where does this leave parents and educators who are considering the adoption of a school-uniform policy? The research on school uniforms forms a shaky foundation for asserting that if we adopt a school uniform for our students a whole host of positive student outcomes will result. As a stand-alone strategy for improvement, there is little research that supports the efficacy of school uniforms as a reform strategy. Perceptions of educators who have adopted uniform policies appear to be the one consistent research outcome. But it must be kept in mind that these educators may have invested in the outcome of the policy. Educators may not notice all student behaviors and "may not report all incidents considering a negative image to the public."[78]

While educators who have adopted school-uniform policies are, on the whole, supportive of the policies, students, not surprisingly, are not. Kneia DaCosta's 2006 study of urban high-school students' reactions to a school-uniform policy supports the contention that students see school uniforms differently than educators.[79] The study found that students, overwhelmingly, were opposed to the uniforms and were noncompliant in the first year of the policy.[80] They developed and employed strategies to undermine the school-uniform policy. Students, as Wade and Safford, among others, point out, see the impact of school uniforms differently and more negatively than their teachers and administrators. Could the push in some schools for implementing casual, nonuniform days be an administrative response to the students' reactions to wearing a uniform?

While the research does not provide strong support for a school uniform, it does not necessarily support the opposite position that a school-uniform policy should not be adopted. Several of the studies above found negative results with wearing school uniforms but, like the studies that found school uniforms to be beneficial, they are not consistent. Younger students, several studies found, may be more receptive to school uniforms, and thus uniforms may positively influence their behavior. There may be valid reasons for a school to adopt a school uniform that are not based on demonstrated student behavior or academic outcomes.

A school may want a particular look and identification for its students and its school. For example, a study in Florida of two county school districts—one with a school-uniform policy and one without—concluded that there was no national or Florida data that showed that "school uniforms significantly impact student achievement or crime or violence."[81] Therefore, the authors of the study found that the current dress-code policy was appropriate. However, the authors noted that wearing school uniforms might enhance other benefits such as school spirit, pride, and a positive culture.

The educators and parents may link school uniforms with a variety of improvement strategies. The multiplier effect of large-scale and comprehensive reform, which uses a broad range of strategies, may include school uniforms as one of its strategies. Jafeth Sanchez, a researcher at the University of Nevada, Reno, commenting in her coauthored study of middle-school perceptions, school violence records, and police records of their first year of a mandatory school-uniform policy, made this observation: "If a simple change in attire can positively influence more than 30 percent, or even 25 percent of a school's student population, then perhaps administrators, teachers and community members find it worth the effort."[82]

Sanchez suggests that because a simple change of clothes has a positive influence on student behavior, then all school communities should seriously consider adopting this reform strategy. But common sense, as well as a wealth of research studies, indicates that the simple mandate requiring students to wear school uniforms cannot by itself create radical changes in a school environment. School uniforms alone are no substitute for the heavy lifting necessary to bring about sustained school improvement. The research to date has not established that school uniforms can be counted on to reduce school violence, improve school attendance, eliminate gang activity, or bring about improved learning outcomes, an esprit de corps among students, or a better school environment. A study of security measures in Texas middle and high schools found that school uniforms were not effective in reducing school-based crimes.[83] Sustained and integrated effort beyond just a change of clothes is necessary to make the promises of school uniforms a reality. School uniforms may play a part, but they must be part of a larger, more comprehensive school-reform strategy.

NOTES

1. Wendell Anderson, "School Dress Codes and Uniform Policies," *Policy Report No. 4: Reporting on Policy Issues in K–12 Educational Management*, ERIC Clearinghouse on Educational Management, 2002, p. 9. Available at https://scholarsbank.uoregon.edu/xmlui/bitstream/handle/1794/3464/dress_code.pdf?sequence=1.
2. Editors, "Dress Codes Help Schools Educate Our Children," *Portsmouth Herald* (Portsmouth, NH), September 8, 2012.
3. Ibid.
4. 240 F.3d 437, 443 (5th Cir. 2001).
5. Valley View Elementary, (n.d.), available at http://www.razoo.com/story/Valleyview.
6. 426 F.3d 419 (9th Cir. 2008).
7. Palmer v. Waxahachie Independent School District, 579 F.3d 502, 511 (5th Cir. 2009).
8. Todd A. DeMitchell, Richard Fossey, and Casey Cobb, "Dress Codes in the Public Schools: Principals, Policies, and Precepts," *Journal of Law & Education* 29 (2000): 31–49.
9. The six questions follow:

    1. I believe that a dress code improves student behavior.
    2. Students do not have a constitutional right to wear clothes of their choice to school.
    3. I believe that a dress code policy prepares students for the realities of the work world once they leave school.
    4. I believe that dress codes are worth the trouble of enforcing.
    5. I believe that dress codes reduce student-to-student sexual harassment.
    6. I support the implementation of a mandatory school uniform policy.

    Ibid., 38–39.
10. Ibid., 42–44.
11. Ibid., 43.
12. Ibid., 44.
13. Ibid., 43–44.
14. Ibid., 41.
15. Ibid., 42.
16. Ibid., 44–45.
17. Ibid., 45.
18. Ibid.
19. Ibid.

20. National Association of Elementary School Principals, *Survey of School Principals Reports Positive Effects of School Uniforms*, February 2000, available at http://www.naesp.org/ContentLoad.do?contentId=929.

21. M. Sue Stanley, "School Uniforms and Safety," *Education and Urban Society* 28, no. 4 (1996): 424.

22. Ibid., 433.

23. Ibid., 432 (emphasis in original).

24. Ibid., 433.

25. Ibid., 434.

26. David L. Brunsma and K. A. Rockquemore, "Effects of Student Uniforms on Attendance, Behavior Problems, Substance Use, and Academic Achievement," *Journal of Educational Research* 92, no. 1 (1998): 53, 54.

27. Ann Bodine, "School Uniforms, Academic Achievement, and Uses of Research," *Journal of Educational Research* 97, no. 2 (2003): 67. However, see David L. Brunsma and K. A. Rockquemore, "Statistics, Sound Bites, and School Uniforms: A Reply to Bodine," *Journal of Educational Research* 97, no. 2 (2003): 72.

28. Paul Barton, Richard J. Coley, and Harold Wenglensky, *The Links Among School Discipline, Student Delinquency, and Academic Achievement* (Princeton, NJ: Educational Testing Service Policy Information Center, 1998), http://education.toodoc.com/doc/23464/ (finding no significant difference for drug use and other delinquency issues); Zollie Stevenson and E. W. Chunn, *Uniform Policy/Dress Codes: School Staff and Parent Perceptions of Need and Impact* (Washington, DC: District of Columbia Public Schools, 1991) (ERIC Document Reproduction Service No. ED 331933).

29. S. Thomas, "Uniforms in the Schools: Proponents Say It Cuts Competition; Others Are Not So Sure," *Black Issues in Higher Education* 11, no. 17 (1994): 44; Kathy S. Samuels, "The Relationship of School Uniforms to Students' Achievement, Attendance, Discipline Referrals and Perceptions: An Analysis of One Urban School District," doctoral dissertation, the University of Alabama, Birmingham, 2003 *Dissertation Abstracts International, 64,* 2734 (UMI No. 3101535); (Student achievement increased [1995–1998], discipline referrals decreased [1994–1999], and average daily attendance increased [1994–1998]).

30. David L. Brunsma, *The School Uniform Movement and What It Tells Us About American Education: A Symbolic Crusade* (Lanham, MD: Scarecrow Education, 2004).

31. Ibid., 45.

32. Ibid., 42.

33. Ibid., 42–43.

34. Ibid., 44–45.

35. Ibid., 180.

36. Ibid., 182.

37. Ibid., 183. Brunsma further wrote, "What is clear from these analyses is that school uniforms, as a policy and strategy, do *not* play a role in producing more parental involvement, increased preparedness, positive approaches toward learning, pro-school attitudes, a heightened feeling of school unity and safety, or positive school climates." Ibid., 195 (emphasis in original).

38. Ryan Yeung, "Are School Uniforms a Good Fit? Results from the ECLS-K and the NELS," *Educational Policy* 23, no. 6 (2009): 847–74. ECLS-K stands for Early Childhood Longitudinal Study-Kindergarten and NELS stands for National Education Longitudinal Study.

39. Ibid., 863. Interestingly, the researcher found, "Children in other religious private schools and private nonreligious schools with uniforms score below their counterparts in these schools that do not require uniforms on both reading and math." Ibid.

40. Ibid., 867. "In the case of reading, science, and history, Catholic school children who are required to wear uniforms to school score below Catholic school children who are not required to wear uniforms to school." Ibid. However, there is a 0.358 increase in math scores for uniforms over no uniform. Ibid.

41. Ibid., 871.

42. Seunghee Han, "A Mandatory Uniform Policy in Urban Schools: Findings from the School Survey on Crime and Safety: 2003–04," *International Journal of Education Policy and Leadership* 5, no. 8 (2010), available at www.ijepl.ca.

43. Ibid., 9.

44. Ibid.

45. Ibid., 8.

46. Ibid., 9.

47. John A. Huss, "The Role of School Uniforms in Creating an Academically Motivating Climate: Do Uniforms Influence Teacher Expectations?" *Journal of Ethnographic and Qualitative Research* 31 (2007): 31–39.

48. Ibid., 38.

49. Ibid., 35.

50. Ibid., 36.

51. Ibid., 37

52. Ibid.

53. Ibid.

54. Ibid.

55. Ibid., 38.

56. Warren A. Hodge and La'Tara Osborne-Lampkin, *An Evaluative Study of Bradford Middle* School *Uniform Policy: Merit, Worth, and Impact*, June 2010, available at http://mybradford.us/PDFs/BMS%20UNIFORM%20STUDY%20JUNE%202010.pdf. The evaluators concluded that the data "do not show a cause and effect relationship between the [school uniform] policy and student achievement." Ibid., 42.

57. Kathy S. Samuels, "The Relationship of School Uniforms to Student Achievement, Attendance, Discipline Referrals and Perceptions: An Analysis of One Urban School District," doctoral dissertation, University of Alabama, Birmingham, 2003.

58. Pamela Y. Hoffler-Riddick, "The Relationship Between the Implementation of a Mandatory Uniform Dress Policy and Attendance, Grade Point Average, and Self-Esteem," dissertation, University of Vermont, 1998, p. 89.

59. Wesley Scott Johnson, "Analyses of the Impact of School Uniforms on Violence in North Carolina Public High Schools," dissertation, East Carolina University, 2010.

60. Ibid., 78.

61. Ibid., 95.

62. Ibid., 110. The largest percentage of disagreement was over the question of school uniforms improving classroom behavior. Seventy percent agreed or strongly agreed while 30 percent disagreed or strongly disagreed.

63. Ibid., 112.

64. Ibid., 115.

65. Kathleen Kiley Wade and Mary E. Stafford, "Public School Uniforms: Effect on Perceptions of Gang Presence, School Climate, and Student Self-Perceptions," *Education and Urban Society*, 35, no. 4 (2003): 399–420.

66. Elisabetta Gentile and Scott A. Imberman, *Dressed for Success? Do School Uniforms Improve Student Behavior, Attendance, and Achievement?* January 15, 2010, available at http://www.utdallas.edu/research/tsp-erc/pdf/seminar_paper_imberman.pdf.

67. Ibid., 21.
68. Ibid., 15.
69. Ibid., 11.
70. Ibid., 14.
71. Ibid., 13.
72. Ibid., 23.
73. Ibid.
74. Bodine, *supra* note 27, 67.
75. Bruce G. Simons-Morton, Aria Davis Crump, Denise L. Haynie, and Keith E. Saylor, "Student-School Bonding and Adolescent Problem Behavior," *Health Education Research: Theory and Practice* 14, no. 1 (1999): 99–107, 102.
76. Executive Apparel, *School Uniforms Will Create a Cohesive Bond among Students*, March 22, 2012, available at http://executiveapparel.com/school-uniforms-will-create-a-cohesive-bond-among-students.
77. Ibid.
78. Han, *supra* note 41, 2.
79. Kneia DaCosta, "Dress Code Blues: An Exploration of Urban Students' Reactions to a Public High School Uniform Policy," *Journal of Negro Education* 75, no. 1 (2006): 49–59.
80. Ibid., 49.
81. Orange County Public Schools, School Uniform Study, (n.d.), available at https://www.ocps.net/es/legislative/Documents/School%20Uniform%20Project%20PP%20(2).pdf.
82. Claudene Wharton, "College of Education Researchers Conduct Study on Impacts of School Uniforms," *Nevada Today*, April 23, 2013, http://www.unr.edu/nevada-today/news/2013/school-uniform-study.
83. Sutham Cherurprakobkit and Robert A. Bartsch, "Security Measures on School Crime in Texas Middle and High Schools," *Educational Research* 47, no. 2 (June 2005): 235–50.

Chapter Six

Policy Implications for Dress Codes and School Uniforms

Balancing Rights and Responsibilities

> If someone wants to do well in school they will without the help of dull and useless pieces of cloth.[1]
>
> —Laura Wicki, responding to an online petition to stop Pinkerton Academy (Derry, New Hampshire) from adopting a school-uniform policy

Should students be able to wear anything they want to school? The consistent answer from everyone, except possibly students, is no. While individuals walking the sidewalks, strolling the public parks, playing on their lawns, or sitting on their front porches may have great latitude in what they choose to wear, students should not have that same unfettered right while at school.

The school is a special place, after all. It is a place of learning and it is a place of business. Crop tops and pajama bottoms that may be tolerated in public need not be tolerated in the classroom. Invitations and advertisements for sexual or illegal activity may have to be accepted on the public boardwalks of our beaches but our public-school hallways are another matter.

Schools not only teach manners and habits of civility, as the Supreme Court noted in its *Fraser* decision; they also prepare students for their entry into an adult workplace where employers may not give workers the unfettered right to choose what they wear. Certainly, private employers, which employ the majority of all American workers, have no constitutional obligation to allow workers the license to choose what they wear during the workday. Can you imagine what a Wells Fargo supervisor would say if a banking employee reported to work wearing a t-shirt proclaiming the joys of promiscuity or advocating the use of illegal drugs?

Thus, it make sense for schools to impose student-dress standards that prepare students for the realities and constraints of adulthood, including an expectation by most employers that employees show up for work appropriately dressed. Students have rights and schools have responsibilities. Finding the balance by properly placing the fulcrum is a challenge for educators.

Moreover, schools can and should monitor the clothing choices of their students to ensure that the learning environment and the social environment of the school are not compromised. Two approaches to this important responsibility are to establish and enforce a dress code that defines the types of student attire that are prohibited at school. Examples include the prohibitions on clothing that contain messages about drugs, alcohol, or violence; identification of gang affiliation and territory; symbols and messages that are likely to create a disturbance; and inappropriate clothing such as revealing or sexually provocative clothes worn by both males and females. Indeed, as we explained in a companion volume, *Dress Codes and the First Amendment: Legal Challenges and Policy Issues*, school dress codes specifying what students can or cannot wear to school are common all over the United States.

The second approach is for schools to define what students *must* wear to school. Schools that take this approach adopt mandatory school-uniform policies. These policies state that only specific color combinations and types of clothing such as collared shirts can be worn to school. All others, whether they carry a message or are just a fashion statement or are what happens to be clean that morning, are banned.

Schools that establish student dress codes and schools that require students to wear school uniforms are taking fundamentally different philosophical approaches about regulating what students wear to school. Dress codes seek to establish an environment free from certain messages and inappropriate clothing choices. School uniforms are designed not only to maintain an appropriate learning environment but also to foster specific student behaviors. Less violence, better attendance, higher academic achievement, greater school cohesion, and school pride are articulated outcomes in many school-uniform policies.

Two other outcomes commonly associated with a school-uniform policy are that it makes the lives of parents easier in the morning by reducing the disagreements about what to wear to school, and it reduces families' clothing budgets—particularly low-income families. These goals are worth tunneling deeper into, first by asking whether a school policy, which school authorities are obligated to enforce, should be aimed at making parenting easier. This is a worthy social consideration, but should a school adopt a policy designed to make the lives of parents easier when such a policy is only marginally related to what the schools do?

Dress codes, on the other hand, do not seek to assist parents in family-clothing choices; they simply try to stop inappropriate attire and accessories from being worn in the classrooms and in school hallways. While both dress codes and school-uniform policies focus on establishing an appropriate learning environment, uniforms posit certain student outcomes that dress codes typically do not assert.

The thesis of school uniforms is that wearing a uniform to school results in increased positive behaviors. But left untested is the reverse thesis: not wearing a school uniform results in certain negative student behaviors that are attributable to students' morning clothing choices.

THE RESEARCH: SCHOOL UNIFORMS

An August 2013 *USA Today* article stated that nearly one in five public schools required uniforms in 2010, despite the fact that there is inconclusive evidence about the impact of school uniforms.[2] How to explain why school uniforms are appearing on the policy agenda of school boards in an era that supposedly grounds policy-making on data-driven decision-making is a challenge. Does policy rhetoric trump reality?

Perhaps, as policy theorist John Kingdon has stated, policy windows open when there is a confluence of three separate policy streams.[3] Problems (school violence and low academic outcomes), proposals (a school uniform), and politics (the desire for a low-cost policy that is easy to implement and is visible) converged to move school uniforms to the forefront of the public-school agenda. When problems and proposals match the attention of participants inside and outside of government, they can move the levers of politics. Without a doubt, multiple forces have converged to put school uniforms on many school boards' policy agendas. Has the introduction of school uniforms improved school climates? Have school uniforms contributed to the creation of safer, more secure school environments that have led to high student achievement?

As set forth in the previous chapter, the research on the effect of school uniforms is mixed. Regarding student academic outcomes, the research does not provide clear support for the thesis that instituting school uniforms produces higher levels of student achievement. Not only is the research on the benefit of school uniforms mixed, some research, primarily using large data sets, has found that school uniforms have a negative impact on academic outcomes.

> The benefits of School Uniforms seem attractive but are difficult to prove.
>
> Source: Pearson, "Uniforms for Learning," *The Learning Curve*, 2014, available at http://thelearningcurve.pearson.com/articles/article/uniforms-for-learning#_ftn3.

If the purpose of a school uniform is to make the school environment safer, the evidence once again is mixed. Some research found some reductions in school violence, while others found no reductions that could not be the result of chance. Interestingly, some of the research on perceptions showed that educators found a positive influence for school uniforms while students reached the opposite conclusion.

As discussed earlier, part of the explanation for the difference of opinion between educators and student can probably be explained by the fact that a school-uniform policy was imposed by school administrators. It seems likely that school administrators are more likely than students to identify with a school-uniform policy that they themselves developed, supported, and implemented. Students, on the other hand, may believe that the policy is restrictive of their choices, and was imposed on them without giving them any voice in the decision. It is the policy choice that students may not have selected to improve their behavior, increase their test scores, or create a more positive school environment. Students and educators view school uniforms through different lenses, and their perceptions and differing conclusions about the efficacy of school uniforms may at least partly be explained by bias.

If there is not a consistent research base to support school uniforms as a strategy to make schools safe and to raise academic achievement, what policy goals are furthered? One of the original policy goals for school uniforms was to level the playing the field for student attire. The competition for what to wear often leaves parents frazzled and educators responding to the disruption over the quality of clothes and occasionally over theft, bullying, and intimidation that relates to school clothing, particularly highly prized and highly priced running shoes. Does a school-uniform policy make it easier for low-income families with limited budgets to provide children with school clothes?

The clothing playing field may be leveled by colors but clearly not by quality. As Stanley noted in chapter 5, some of the negative student behaviors that school administrators saw in Long Beach were attributed to old, faded, and worn-out school uniforms. There is logic to Stanley's assertion that low-income families are disadvantaged when their children's school clothing gets old and they cannot afford to purchase new clothing at needed intervals. And this is true whether or not children from low-income families wear uniforms to school.

Two Jackson County, Georgia middle schools were poised to adopt school uniforms for the 2012–2013 school year. A parent asked the school board to reverse the decision about implementing the school-uniform policy, arguing that the new policy would be too expensive for low-income families, as students would have to purchase two sets of clothing—uniforms to wear during the school day and other clothing when they were not at school. The mandatory uniform policy was delayed indefinitely.[4] The argument that school uniforms will save parents money was rejected in Georgia.

After reviewing the research on school uniforms, we find it conflicted. There is no clear body of research that states that school uniforms lead to reduced school violence, improved student behavior, better attendance, a more conducive learning environment, higher motivation, or better learning outcomes. This does not mean that schools should not adopt a school-uniform policy. It means that the research does not provide strong support if a school uniform is adopted as a stand-alone policy to meet these goals. On the other hand, a school-uniform policy adopted as part of an overall strategy of reform may be effective. For example, adopting school uniforms to help create an image that a school wants to present to the internal and external world may be effective. We strongly caution educators, school boards, parents, and communities to carefully consider the purpose that uniformed students will serve. Adopting school uniforms without introducing other policies to improve the school environment will probably not produce any meaningful change.

STUDENT CLOTHING CHOICES AND THE CONSTITUTION

In the public school setting, the First Amendment protects the nondisruptive expression of ideas. It does not erect a shield that handicaps the proper functioning of the public schools.

Source: Sypniewski v. Warren Hills Regional Board of Education, 307 F.3d 243, 259 (3d Cir. 2002), *cert. denied*, 538 U.S. 1033 (2002).

Dress Codes

Jurisprudence on students' free-expression rights has traveled a long road since the Supreme Court's *Tinker* decision in 1969. The Court's guiding principle, that students have a constitutional right to engage in nondisruptive free speech, has been invoked in support of student demands to wear earrings, bracelets with messages, sagging pants, cross-dressing for their prom, and T-shirts with lewd or disruptive messages. The outcome has been mixed. Dress-code litigation tends to look more like potpourri than a unified, articulated body of case law. As we explained in our earlier book, unanimity on the issue of the constitutionality of dress codes has not been achieved, leaving a large degree of uncertainty both in the courts and in the principal's office.

Lawsuits by students challenging dress codes because of a desire to wear whatever they want ill serves the school and society.[5] First, it trivializes the Constitution and the courts for judges to analyze a student's right to wear sagging pants as an expression of individuality or a sexually suggestive T-shirt to school under principles adopted in the *Tinker* decision, a case involving serious political speech. Not all conduct within the schoolhouse gate should be labeled as speech that deserves the full panoply of constitutional protection. The public school is a special place, reserved for learning, and rules regulating speech in the public square may not be appropriate for regulating speech in the classrooms of the public schools.

Second, litigation over student dress codes may discourage local educators from making the commonsense decisions we expect them to make concerning children's welfare. Whether a lawsuit has merit or not, the possibility of a civil-rights suit over a dress-code provision may intimidate school administrators from adopting regulations designed to maintain a safe and orderly learning environment. For example, how eager will South Hadley school authorities be to adopt a new student-conduct regulation, having experienced protracted litigation over their efforts to ban "Coed Naked" T-shirts?[6] Courts should acknowledge the special characteristics of the schools as discussed in *Tinker*, and give deference (under *Fraser*) to the school officials tasked with the twin responsibilities of securing student constitutional rights and securing and maintaining an appropriate educational environment.

Third, dress-code litigation subverts a primary goal of public education, which is to instill a decent respect for community values and civil speech.[7] That mission, the Supreme Court instructed us, includes the duty to inculcate civic values and promote civil discourse. Outside of those student behaviors that are truly expressive conduct on religious, political, or social issues, students who disagree with the wording of a dress code are free to lobby the school board to change the policy.

This is consistent with the procedures used in other situations, such as curricular decisions, when citizens disagree with the discretionary decision of a school board. What message do children learn about civic responsibility when they discover that their preferences for sagging pants, lewd T-shirts, or clothes that make them feel good are entitled to the same constitutional scrutiny that the Tinker children received when they protested, with courage and dignity, the Vietnam War? Also, as the judge in the *Pyle* noted, dress codes can protect students from "an environment of unrelenting winks, snickering, and sexual prodding."[8]

Students have constitutional rights, such as the right to free speech, that public-school educators are charged with protecting. Those rights must be protected. However, we are mindful that the Supreme Court in *Tinker*, which articulated the free-speech rights of students, also raised a caution that the symbolic speech of the Tinkers' "does not relate to regulation of the length of skirts or the type of clothing or deportment."[9] The court affirmed the "comprehensive authority of the States and the school officials, consistent with fundamental safeguards, to prescribe and control conduct in the schools."[10] Similarly, Justice Harlan stated in his dissent in *Tinker* that he was "reluctant to believe that there is any disagreement between the majority and [himself] on the proposition that school officials should be accorded the widest authority in maintaining discipline and good order in their institutions."[11]

Consequently, we do not believe that the right to free speech should trump reasonable school regulations designed to support an orderly learning environment for all students. We believe that schools, students, and the courts will be best served by a policy of judicial restraint toward school dress regulations. School administrators are best situated to determine the reasonableness of a dress code and whether student expression is lewd, indecent, or offensive regardless of whether the speech is disruptive. As the court held in *Tinker*, First Amendment rights for students are "applied in light of the special characteristics of the school environment."[12]

Decisions by administrators that punish speech that they personally do not agree with and that is not tied to a reasonable standard such as a legitimate pedagogical concern[13] should give rise to judicial intervention. Maintaining order and a civil atmosphere should be the guiding principle for reasonable dress-code regulations. Absent a showing of unreasonableness, judicial scrutiny should be limited. The Constitution is well served by this parsimonious view and the reasonable control of schools resides with its administrators and elected board members.

Reasonable school dress codes define boundaries that students will likely encounter in the work world. It is acceptable to provide latitude to students but license is another matter. The classroom is a work environment for students and educators. To expect that students' and educators' attire reflect the importance of that work environment is not unreasonable.

Dress regulations that target lewd, vulgar, or sexual language (*Fraser*) on attire; scanty clothing; bedroom and beach wear; promotions for drugs, alcohol (*Morse*), and tobacco; and dangerous objects like chains and dog collars are reasonable and consistent with the *in loco parentis* responsibility. These are the types of clothing that parents would, could, and should prohibit their children from wearing to school. Attire that creates or is likely to create a material and substantial disruption (*Tinker*), such as attire with the Confederate flag, should also be banned. Educators have a responsibility to create, support, and to maintain the environment of the school, educating students to be productive citizens of society.

Students should be afforded flexibility, not license, of expression of who they are. They may well often approach the boundaries of reasonableness of attire, just as they do with their actions. It is the responsibility of educators to define and enforce those responsibilities clearly and consistently. This well serves students and the community. This also requires that the courts provide the legal direction that assists educators in knowing where to set the boundary in order to comport with the constitutional rights that students enjoy. A clear standard addressing the constitutional rights of public schools to choose their school attire articulated by the Supreme Court would go a long way in bringing a greater level of certainty to dress codes.

We raised the specter of dress codes moving closer to school uniforms by adopting the standard used in *Palmer v. Waxahachie Independent School District*, which we discussed in chapter 4. In this case, Paul Palmer, a high-school sophomore, sued the Waxahachie School District, claiming the school district's dress code, which prohibited all messages on students' clothing except the school logo, abridged his free-speech rights.[14] The Fifth Circuit rejected Palmer's challenge, ruling that the restrictive dress code was content-neutral, treating all messages the same without regard to their content. Moreover, the court pointed out, there was no evidence to show that the school district had adopted its restrictive student dress policy for the purpose of abridging students' free-speech rights.

The Fifth Circuit's reasoning in the *Palmer* case is similar to the decisions by other federal courts regarding school-uniform policies. In fact, the legal analysis used in the *Palmer* case is almost identical to the analysis used in school-uniform cases. In the *Palmer* case as well as the school-uniform cases, the courts relied heavily on the Supreme Court's decision in *United States v. O'Brien*, in which the Supreme Court upheld a content-neutral regulation that was not adopted for the purpose of abridging free speech and that restricted speech no more than was necessary to meet the regulation's reasonable governmental objective.[15]

The Fifth Circuit's *Palmer* decision explicitly upheld a school district's student dress code based on a constitutional analysis that has consistently been approved by federal courts in school uniform cases. The Waxahachie School District's student dress code controls messages that could be considered lewd or vulgar, advertisements for banned substances, and divisive and disruptive symbols. It relegates speech to small portions of attire such as buttons, pins, and bracelets. *Palmer* may well provide a constitutional avenue for restricting clothing choices for those who seek such a path.

School Uniforms

Thus far, students have been more successful in challenging student dress codes than mandatory school-uniform policies. The paradox is that students have some success contesting the lesser restrictions of a dress code and virtually no success in overturning the more restrictive mandatory school-uniform policies through a constitutional challenge.

So far, the courts seem willing to give school uniforms the chance to transform our schools. And since the courts have ruled consistently that mandatory school-uniform policies are constitutional while ruling less consistently with regard to student dress codes that give students more latitude about what they wear to school, some school administrators may conclude that they are on stronger legal ground imposing a school-uniform policy than trying to enforce a more lenient student dress code that is less likely to be upheld by a federal court.

Nevertheless, a constitutionally firm policy is not the same thing as an educationally sound policy. School reform involves heavy lifting; are school-uniform policies up to the task? Before adopting a mandatory school uniform, school districts should review the research on school uniforms; and they should also consider the following challenges.[16]

1. Enforcement. School-uniform policies, as noted above, must be enforced, just like dress-code policies. It can be argued that with a dress code an educator can be selectively blind to dress that may marginally violate the school's student dress policy—a schoolgirl's skirt, for example, may be only a half inch out of compliance. Given the large variation in student dress on any given day, a student violating a school's rules on student attire may just melt into the crowd. However, if there is uniformity to the students' appearance—all khaki and blue, for example, an Aloha shirt will stand out and will require an administrative response. Failure to enforce a school-uniform policy undermines the policy in a very visible way. Thus, school uniforms may require more administrative time to enforce than a simple student dress code.[17]

2. Waivers. School-uniform policies often allow for waivers for such reason as religion or other philosophical reasons. What constitutes a bona fide waiver is the initial question. In November of 2002, the Commissioner of Education for the State of Texas handed down a decision on whether a philosophically grounded reason, not a religious reason, for requesting a waiver from wearing a mandatory school uniform was bona fide. The parents presented the following argument.

> I believe learning to live with ethnic, racial, and a social difference is a big part of growing and maturing. I also believe we need to celebrate these differences and not try to force everyone to conform to one standard. I think Natalia School District's diversity is one of its assets in teaching our children this important life lesson. I believe this lesson would greatly benefit my son after school when he enters the real world.[18]

Essentially the parent believed that diversity was an important social good that should be supported in the public school and that school uniforms stifled diversity. The commissioner found that the parent had a bona fide philosophical objection to his child wearing a school uniform. Furthermore, the commissioner found the school district's denial of the waiver to be "arbitrary, capricious and not supported by substantial evidence."[19]

The issue of religious exemptions for student attire policies is thorny but an important issue to address. Religion is a powerful force in the lives of individuals. A student's religious sensibilities must be approached with sensitivity and without regard to the particularities of a religious tenet. Farida Ali posses the challenge in the following way:

> Students' ability to wear religious attire and symbols in the public school context makes sense because it encourages students to discuss and respond thoughtfully to the religious opinions of others, while eliminating the burden that forces students to choose between their duty to God and their duty to the state and its laws.[20]

Accommodating families who have religious or philosophical objections creates administrative challenges for school authorities who must articulate clear policies for determining which students are entitled to waivers. This adds another level of complexity to administering a school-uniform policy.

For example, in Sierra Vista Junior High School, it was reported that the first ten minutes of class were used trying to figure out who had waivers and who had to be sent to the principal's office for discipline.[21] The head of the math department, Beth Shedd, described the school-uniform policy in the following manner: "It was nuts; it became a huge distraction. It increased friction, it increased discipline problems, having to worry about who was wearing what. It wasn't worth the fight."[22]

In spite of the complexity of working through how wearing a *hijab* or a Star of David necklace or any other religious exemption (piercings for example) fits into the school-uniform policy or the dress code, school officials must take on the task if they are to protect the constitutional rights of their students.[23] Policies on student attire do not automatically render student religious beliefs and practices null and void inside the schoolhouse gate.

The conflict between the appropriateness of religious symbols and dress in the public square as well as the role of religious values and principles is not confined to the public schools. The public school is the brightly polished mirror for this and other conflicts within our society. While writ small in the local public school, these issues represent larger social forces that seek to define the values, practices, and accommodations of our society.

3. Alternative Speech. As seen under *O'Brien*, schools with school-uniform policies must provide students with some alternative methods of speech. The methods may include buttons, bracelets, pins, and perhaps pendants. Of course, allowing students wearing uniforms to proclaim messages on pendants or pins and buttons raises the same problems that schools face when they try to enforce student dress codes.

For example, will a school with a school-uniform policy allow students to wear bracelets that proclaim "I ♥ boobies"? What size button or pin will be allowed? Are Confederate flag pins acceptable, or pins expressing opposition to abortion? Will educators have to write and enforce a parallel dress-code section?

Allowing student expression and mandating a school uniform may create a conundrum for school administrators. If part of the argument for a school uniform is identification with the school, and particularly if the school uniform has the school's name, will individuals interpret a student's message that appears on her/his school uniform as being a message approved or endorsed by the school? For example, will a student's pin that proclaims that homosexuality is a sin be allowed as personal expression on the student's school uniform? School uniforms, by design, are intended to publically identify the student with the school. Consequently, it can be argued that anything that the school allows to be worn on its uniform conveys the position of the school.

4. Elementary, Middle, or High School: Is There a Difference? Does the level of the school make a difference when implementing a school-uniform policy? Is it easier to implement a school uniform at the elementary-school level than at the high-school level?[24] We noted some of the differentiation in free speech between elementary-school-age children and older children in our book *Student Dress Codes and the First Amendment: Legal Challenges and Policy Issues*.[25]

There is a reason that more elementary schools have implemented school-uniform policies than high schools; they are easier to implement at the elementary level than at the secondary level, particularly at the high-school level. DeMitchell, Fossey, and Cobb's study of dress codes and school uniforms supports this conclusion. They found that middle-school principals were significantly more likely to support student uniforms than high-school principals.[26] The NCES 2011–2012 study of safety and security measures discussed earlier in the book reported that in 2011–2012, 20.3 percent of elementary schools required students to wear a school uniform as compared to 12.2 percent of secondary schools.

Secondary-school administrators considering the adoption of a school-uniform policy should consider why this disparity of adoption between levels of schools exists and whether there is a political will and a well-reasoned and presented rationale for implementing the school uniform in their high school. Bare assertions of benefits are unlikely to persuade high-school students who want the liberty to make their own clothing choices.

5. Uniform-Free Days. It is peculiar that so many of the schools that have school uniforms provide uniform-free days. In some cases these days are billed as a reward. If uniforms result in certain positive behaviors, why is it that occasionally those good behaviors are not as important? Does dress-down Friday mean we don't expect as much today from students on the last day of the school week?

We have not heard of dress-code-free days as a reward for good behavior. To use the "4 Bs" description of Winnacunnet High School's dress code, "No bellies, butt, breasts, or boxers,"[27] no amount of good behavior is going to result in suspension of that rule. If wearing a school uniform is important to bring about specific goals, it should be required every day. Does a school's student-uniform policy lose its utility and its credibility when it is not consistently required? In our view, to regularly schedule school-uniform-free days muddles the message about the value of school uniforms.

6. Political Heat. School-uniform policies generate a fair amount of political heat. School districts would be well advised to seek community and educator input early and often before implementing a school-uniform policy. As we have discussed throughout the book, the politics swirling around school-uniform policies are often contentious, and school administrators would be wise not to assume that the adoption of a school-uniform policy can be achieved without controversy.

7. Adult Uniforms. Anticipate the question that First Amendment ombudsman Paul McMasters advanced. He stated, "If school officials think that school uniforms are such a great idea, then they should wear uniforms also."[28] If wearing a school uniform is transformative for students, the argument goes, why wouldn't it also reap benefits for adults at school—identification with the school, better attendance, esprit de corps, easy identification between adult visitors/intruders? While not requiring school employees to wear uniforms, Tennessee recently passed a state law requiring school districts to adopt regulations "that professional employees dress in a manner that maintains respect, establishes credibility as a professional employee as an authority figure and a positive role model."[29]

CONSIDERATIONS AND CONCLUSION

We are not advocating for student uniforms in the public schools, but we believe that school authorities should take the following issues into account before adopting a student-uniform policy:

POLITICAL CONSIDERATIONS

a. Expect resistance. Change is threatening and schools should expect at least some parents to consider school uniforms to be a threat to their right to make their own decisions about what their children wear to school.
b. Involve parents early and throughout the process. Do not leave the public out of this public-education decision.
c. Make sure that you have worked with the faculty, staff, and administrators to answer their questions, to listen carefully to them, and to look for advocates within the schools. What exactly are the problems that school uniforms are intended to address and why do you think, beyond mere speculation and hope, that a school uniform will appropriately and adequately address those concerns?
d. Keep your school board advised at every stage of the school-uniform adoption process. School-board members will face the same type of public scrutiny and heat that the school administration will face. Are board members supportive of the proposed policy? If not, address their concerns before going too far down the implementation road. What do they need to know? Make sure school-board members can publically articulate an educational justification for mandating school uniforms.

ORGANIZATIONAL CONSIDERATIONS

a. Gather research studies that look at both the pros and cons of school-uniform policies. Develop readable position statements for adopting or for not adopting a school-uniform policy based on research and public input. Make those findings easily available prior to community meetings.

b. Know the case law on school uniforms and have it handy for responding to questions.
c. Ensure that there are multiple venues that allow for community input.
d. Make sure that your meetings are well organized and well run. Choose your moderator carefully. It is best to select someone without a position in the discussion.
e. Parents are conscious of the cost of school uniforms. They must provide two sets of clothes, those for school (the uniform) and those for out-of-school activities. What allowances can be made for parents who have reasonable financial constraints and considerations about purchasing a uniform? What are some of the local costs of the uniform?
f. Be wary of specifying particular suppliers for uniforms. Requiring that school uniforms be purchased from a specific retailer reduces options for parents with limited economic means.

LEGAL CONSIDERATIONS

a. What exemptions/opt-out provisions will you allow? As we reviewed in *Frudden v. Pilling* in chapter 4, you should include a carefully crafted exemption for religious reasons. A school-uniform policy may substantially burden the free exercise of a student's religion. Allowing yarmulkes for Jews and headscarves for female students who are practicing Muslims is a good start in crafting religious exemptions.
b. In light of the discussion of noneducation cases in chapter 3, what alternative means of expression will you allow for student speech if students are required to wear uniforms? Will you allow pins, buttons, sashes, or caps? Are there topics that you will not allow to be worn at school (think dress-code restrictions)? Will you allow sagging uniforms similar to *Bivens*? Will you allow students to wear pins that proclaim their opposition to abortion, homosexuality, or the school-uniform policy itself?
c. Given the decision in *Frudden*, will your school uniform include the school's motto, the school's name, or just be blank with no written words? The Fruddens objected to being required to wear the school's motto because it allegedly celebrated leadership over followership and because they disagreed with the motto's claim that the school is likely to produce tomorrow's leaders.[30]

The school's mascot as part of the school uniform, at this point, seems to be safe. However, out of an abundance of caution, the school may want to consider making the mascot and the logo optional, with students being able to purchase patches to affix to their uniform.

As stated above, we are not advocating for school uniforms but we are not lobbying against them either. However, as we have just outlined, the road to adopting a school-uniform policy is fraught with peril and school administrators who attempt to implement such a policy would be wise to prepare for opposition.

Currently, research does not support the belief that school uniforms lead to positive academic and behavioral outcomes in the school environment. Bringing about changes in student behavior, attitudes, responsibilities, and academic performance is more complicated than wearing blue and khaki rather than jeans and a New England Patriots or New Orleans Saints T-shirt. In our estimation, just requiring a change in clothes is a poor strategy for bringing about substantive change in a school. Alone, it is an inadequate substitute for real change efforts. Combined with other strategies, implementing a school-uniform policy may be an effective strategy for changing a school's culture.

Dress codes designed to define the boundaries of acceptable student attire are an important means for maintaining an orderly school environment and for defending the boundaries of modesty, cleanliness, and civic behavior. Even though dress codes have occasionally been challenged in court, no court has ruled that schools have no legitimate interest in regulating students' clothing choices.

> Judge Posner wrote: "Public Schools have an interest of constitutional dignity in being allowed to manage their affairs and shape their destiny free of minute supervision by federal judges and juries."
>
> Source: *Brandt v. Board of Education of City of Chicago*, 480 F.3d 460, 467 (7th Cir. 2007).

School-uniform policies are generally implemented to achieve broader and more sweeping educational goals than dress codes. Often they are introduced as a means of transforming a school culture in order to obtain higher levels of academic achievement and reduce incidents of student misconduct.

But research does not support the thesis that schools can be transformed simply through the introduction of mandatory school uniforms.

Coupled with other school-reform strategies, school uniforms may play a role in reshaping a school's culture and creating a school environment that is perceived as more orderly and more focused on academics. But implemented in isolation, school uniforms offer a vain hope and false promise of change and will likely produce disappointing results unless they are introduced as part of a wider and encompassing effort to achieve change.

The lessons of the politics of adopting a school-uniform policy must not be lost on educators and parents who pursue such a policy. Parents have to be involved early and throughout the process. It is not just the law that can derail a policy of reform; uninformed political action that leaves the public out of the deliberations of its public schools also causes reform to jump the tracks. Sound politics, based on legal precedents and supported by research, combine to inform good policy decisions.

NOTES

1. See Change.org, Pinkerton Academy, *"Unified Dress Code" (Uniforms): Stop the Uniform Proposal*, 2013, available at https://www.change.org/petitions/pinkerton-academy-unified-dress-code-uniforms-stop-the-uniform-proposal .
2. Greg Toppo, "What to Wear? Schools Increasingly Making That Decision," *USA Today*, August 18, 2013, http://www.usatoday.com/story/news/nation/2013/08/18/more-school-uniforms/2662387/ .
3. John W. Kingdon, *Agendas, Alternatives, and Public Policies*, 2nd ed. (New York: Longman, 2010).
4. "Schools Drop Uniform Dress Code Policy for Next School Year," *Jackson Herald Today*, June 22, 2012, http://www.jacksonheraldtoday.com/archives/7256-Schools-drop-uniform-dress-code-policy-for-next-school-year.html .
5. The following discussion is based on our earlier volume, Richard Fossey and Todd A. DeMitchell, *Student Dress Codes and the First Amendment: Legal Challenges and Policy Issues* (Lanham, MD: Rowman & Littlefield, 2014).
6. Legal expenses in the [*Pyle*] case to date total around $30,000, according to Norman Guertin, administrative assistant to the Board of Selectmen. William A. Davis, "When the Shirt Hits the Fan," *Boston Globe*, January 10, 1996, p. 28.
7. Bethel School District No. 403 v. Fraser, 478 U.S. 675 (1986).
8. Pyle v. South Hadley School Committee, 861 F. Supp. 157, 170 (D. Mass. 1994)
9. Tinker v. Des Moines Independent Community School District, 393 U.S. 503, 507–8 (1969).
10. Ibid., 507.
11. Ibid., 525 (Harlan, J., dissenting).
12. Ibid., 506.
13. Hazelwood School District v. Kuhlmeier, 484 U.S. 260 (1988).
14. Palmer v. Waxahachie Independent School District, 579 F.3d 502 (5th Cir. 2009).

15. 391 U.S. 367 (1968).

16. These observations are informed by Todd A. DeMitchell and Mark A. Paige, "School Uniforms in the Public Schools: Symbol or Substance? A Law and Policy Analysis," *Education Law Reporter* 250 (2010): 847.

17. For example, a public-school teacher, Vasiliki Partinoudi, in New England captured the challenge of clothing choice and policy response. She noted that while she favors school uniforms because "they can promote school safety, improve discipline, and enhance the learning environment," she prefers a dress code even though it is harder to enforce. Vasiliki Partinoudi, communication, October 30, 2014. Permission granted by Ms. Partinoudi on October 30, 2014 (statement on file with Todd DeMitchell).

18. Benjamin B. v. Natalia Independent School District, Docket No. 008-R5-901, Commissioner of Education, State of Texas, November 5, 2002, p. 4.

19. Ibid., 6.

20. Farida Ali, "Students' Religious Liberty: Religious Attire and Symbols in American Public Schools," *Rutgers Journal of Law & Religion* 15, no. 1 (2013): 32.

21. Kate Zernicke, "Plaid's Out Again, as Schools Give Up Requiring Uniforms," *New York Times*, September 13, 2002, http://www.nytimes.com/2002/09/13/us/plaid-s-out-again-as-schools-give-up-requiring-uniforms.html .

22. Ibid. By the spring of 2002, only two hundred students of the 1,300 wore the school uniform. In addition, the school allowed casual Fridays, but eventually abandoned the policy of requiring a school uniform.

23. See Menora v. Illinois High School Association, 683 F.2d 1030 (7th Cir. 1982), in which the Seventh Circuit Court of Appeals vacated a lower court's order that upheld a school policy banning a Jewish student from wearing a *yarmulke* (the ban was on all headgear) in a high school for safety reasons. The appellate court ruled that such a ban violated the Free Exercise rights of the student. The Seventh Circuit ordered that the student be allowed to try to fashion a way to keep the yarmulke secure. If no remedy that meets the conflicting interests of safety and Jewish law could be found, the Seventh Circuit, concluded, the student would have to choose between two options, playing basketball or following his religion. Ibid., 1035.

24. Dennis L. Evans, "School Uniforms: An Unfashionable Dissent," *NASSP Bulletin* 80 (1996): 115–16. ("To begin with, the programs that have gained parental support, media attention and thus, political advocacy are, for the most part, found in elementary schools where the age of the children dictates that the problems school uniforms allegedly solve do not exist to any significant degree in the first place. . . . [S]chool uniforms simply don't work at the high school level").

25. Fossey and DeMitchell, *Student Dress Codes and the First Amendment*, chap. 2.

26. Todd A. DeMitchell, Richard Fossey, and Casey Cobb, "Dress Codes in the Public Schools: Principals, Policies, and Precepts," *Journal of Law & Education* 29, no. 1 (2000): 31, 41.

27. E-mail communication discussing the "4Bs" dress code in the possession of coauthor DeMitchell from Ashley Mancusi (January 16, 2013). Arkansas, in March of 2011, signed into law HB 1936 An Act to Require School Districts to Prohibit the Wearing of Clothing that Exposes Underwear, Buttocks, or the Breast of a female student; and for Purposes (Arkansas Code § 6-18-503). The Legislative Intent asserted that prohibiting these three activities "will prevent disruptions in the learning environment, advance the education of students, enhance the preparation of students to enter the workforce, and make disruptive incidents of violence less likely to occur." Available at ftp://www.arkleg.state.ar.us/Bills/2011/Public/HB1936.pdf .

28. David L. Hudson Jr., *The Silencing of Student Voices: Preserving Free Speech in America's Schools* (Nashville, TN: First Amendment Center, 2003), 62.

29. The bill was introduced on December 15, 2011 and signed into law on May 9, 2012. HB 2222 107th Regular Session (2011–2012), available at http://www.capitol.tn.gov/Bills/107/Bill/SB2547.pdf .

30. Debra Cassens Weiss, "School Uniform with 'Tomorrow's Leaders' Motto Amount to Compelled Speech, 9th Circuit Says," *ABA Journal*, February 18, 2014, http://www.abajournal.com/news/article/school_uniforms_with_tomorrows_leaders_motto_amount_to_compelled_speech_9th/ .

Court Case Citations by Chapter

FEDERAL COURTS

United States Supreme Court	Chapter(s)
Abington School District v. Schempp	2
Abood v. Detroit Board of Education	4
Adler v. Board of Education	2
Beauharnais v. Illinois	2
Bethel School District No. 403 v. Fraser	Preface, 2, 3, 4, 6
Board of Education v. Earls	2
Board of Education, Island Trees Union Free School District No. 26 v. Pico	1
Brandenburg v. Ohio	2
Brown v. Board of Education	2
Chaplinsky v. New Hampshire	2
Cohen v. California	2
Cornelius v. NAACP	Preface, 4
Gilbert v. State of Minnesota	2
Goss v. Lopez	2
Grayned v. City of Rockford	1
Hague v. CIO	3

Hazelwood School District v. Kuhlmeier	Preface, 2, 3, 4, 6
Ingraham v. Wright	2
Lamb's Chapel v. Center Moriches Free School District	Preface
Linmark Associates, Inc. v. Town of Willingboro	2
Lovell v. City of Griffin	2
McIntyre v. Ohio Elections Commission	2
Menora v. Illinois High School Association	6
Miller v. California	2
Morse v. Frederick	Preface
New Jersey v. T.L.O.	2
New York v. Ferber	2
New York Times Co. v. Sullivan	2
Palko v. Connecticut	2
Perry Educational Association v. Perry Local Educator's Association	Preface, 2
Plyler v. Doe	1
Poulos v. New Hampshire	2
R.A.V. v. St. Paul	
Riley v. National Federation of the Blind, Inc.	4
Shelton v. Tucker	2
Simon & Shuster, Inc. v. Members of the New York State Crime Victims Board	2
Spence v. Washington	Preface, 3, 4
Terminello v. Chicago	2
Texas v. Johnson	Preface, 2, 3, 4
Tinker v. Des Moines Independent Community School District	Preface, 1, 2, 3, 4, 6
United States v. O'Brien	Preface, 3, 4, 6
United States v. Schwimmer	2

Vernonia School District 47J. v. Acton	2
Virginia v. Black	2
Ward v. Rock Against Racism	2
West Virginia State Board of Education v. Barnette	Preface, 3,4
Whitney v. California	Preface
Wooley v. Maynard	4

Federal Court of Appeals (Circuit)	**Chapter(s)**
B.H. v. Easton Area School District (3d)	Preface, 1, 3
Blau v. Fort Thomas Public School District (6th Cir.)	2, 3, 4
Boroff v. Van Wert City Board of Education (6th Cir.)	1, 2
Brandt v. Board of Education of City of Chicago (7th Cir.)	2, 4, 6
Burnside v. Byars (5th Cir.)	2
Canady v. Bossier Parish School Board (5th Cir.)	4, 5
Frederick v. Morse (9th Cir.)	2
Frudden v. Pilling (9th Cir.)	Preface, 4, 6
Jacobs v. Clark County School District (9th Cir.)	Preface, 1, 3, 4, 5
Karr v. Schmidt (5th Cir.)	4
LaVine v. Blaine School District (9th Cir.)	Preface, 2
Littlefield v. Forney Independent School District (5th Cir.)	4
Morgan v. Swanson (5th Cir.)	2
Morrison v. Board of Education of Boyd County (6th Cir.)	2
Newsome v. Albemarle County School Board (4th Cir.)	2
Nuxoll v. Indian Prairie Independent School District (7th Cir.)	2

Palmer v. Waxahachie Independent School District (5th Cir.)	2, 3, 4, 5, 6
Pickup v. Brown (9th Cir.)	1
Richards v. Thurston (1st Cir.)	2, 4
Saxe v. State College Area School District (3d Cir.)	2
Sypniewski v. Warren Hills Regional Board of Education (3d)	3, 6

Federal District Court (State)	**Chapter(s)**
A.H. v. Northside Independent School District (TX)	1
Bear v. Fleming (SD)	Preface, 3
Bivens v. Albuquerque Public Schools (NM)	Preface, 2, 3
Broussard v. School Board of Norfolk (VA)	3
Chalifoux v. New Caney Independent School District (TX)	4
Dariano v. Morgan Hill Unified School District	Preface
Denno v. School Board of Volusia County (FL)	Preface, 2
DePinto v. Bayonne Board of Education (NJ)	3, 4
Derry v. Marion Community Schools (IN)	1, 4
Fowler v. Williamson (NC)	4
Frederick v. Morse (AK)	2
Frudden v. Pilling (NV)	4
Governor Wentworth Regional School District v. Hendrickson (NH)	3
Grzywna Ex Rel. Doe v. Schenectady Central Sch. Dist. (NY)	3
Hansen v. Ann Arbor Public Schools (MI)	2
Hicks v. Halifax County Board of Education (NC)	4
Iacono v. Croom (NC)	3
Isaacs v. Board of Education (MD)	3, 4

Jeglin v. San Jacinto Unified School District (CA)	3
K.J. v. Sauk Prairie School District (WI)	Preface, 3
Long v. Board of Education of Jefferson County (KY)	3, 4
Lowry v. Watson Chapel School District (AR)	4
McIntire v. Bethel School District (OK)	3
Morrison v. Board of Education of Boyd County (KY)	2
Pyle By and Through Pyle v. South Hadley School Committee (MA)	Preface, 1, 2, 6
Swany v. San Ramon Valley Unified School District (CA)	1, 3
Vines v. Board of Education of Zion School District No. 6 (IL)	4

STATE COURTS

Case	**Chapter**
Byars v. City of Waterbury (CT)	4
Phoenix Elementary School District No.1 v. Green (AZ)	Preface, 4

Index

About the Authors

Todd A. DeMitchell (BA, La Verne College; MAT, University of La Verne; MA, University of California, Davis; EdD, University of Southern California; Postdoctorate, Harvard University) spent eighteen years in the public schools in California serving as a substitute teacher, elementary-school teacher, assistant principal (K–6), principal (K–8), director of personnel and labor relations (K–12), and superintendent (K–8). Currently, he is the John and H. Irene Peters Professor of Education in the Education Department and the Justice Studies Program, and Faculty Fellow in the Office of Outreach and Academic Engagement at the University of New Hampshire. He has served as associate chair and chair of the Education Department as well as serving as the Chair of the Faculty Senate. The University of New Hampshire selected him as Distinguished Professor. In addition, he received a teaching excellence award, was named Kimball Fellow in the Education Department, named Lamberton Professor of Justice Studies, and he received a research award from the New England Educational Research Organization.

His research focuses on school law and labor relations. This is his seventh book and his fifth book with Rowman & Littlefield Education. His previous books with Rowman & Littlefield include *Student Dress Codes and the First Amendment: Legal Challenges and Policy Issues* (coauthored with Richard Fossey, 2014); *The Limits of Law-Based School Reform: Vain Hopes and False Promises* (coauthored with Richard Fossey, 1997); *Negligence: What Principals Need to Know about Avoiding Liability* (2006); and *Labor Relations in Education: Policies, Politics, and Practices* (2010). He has published over 170 law reviews, book chapters, peer-reviewed articles, and commentaries. His publications have appeared in such journals as *Southern California Interdisciplinary Law Journal*, *Journal of College and University Law*, *Cardozo Public Law, Policy, and Ethics Journal*, *Boston University Public Interest Law Journal*, *Connecticut Public Interest Law Journal*, *Education and Law Journal* (Canada), *Brigham Young University Education and Law Journal*, and the *Journal of Law & Education*.

Richard Fossey (BA, Oklahoma State University; MA University of Texas, Austin; JD, University of Texas School of Law, Austin; EdD, Harvard University) is the Paul Burdin Endowed Professor of Education at the University of Louisiana at Lafayette. Previously, he was professor and Mike Moses Endowed Chair in Educational Leadership at the University of North Texas, Professor and Chair at the University of Houston, and professor and associate dean at Louisiana State University. Prior to joining the academy, he practiced law in Alaska for nine years, primarily representing school districts.

He served on the board of directors of the Education Law Association from 2004 to 2007. In 2014, he received the M. A. McGhehy award from the Education Law Association. He is editor of *Catholic Southwest* and serves on the editorial advisory committee of *West's Education Law Reporte*r. He has written numerous articles and book chapters on education law and policy. His books include *Crime on Campus: Legal Issues and Campus Administration* (coauthored with Michael C. Smith); *Condemning Students to Debt: College Loans and Public Policy* (coedited with Mark Bateman); *Sexual Orientation, Public Schools, and the Law* (coauthored with Todd A. DeMitchell and Suzanne Eckes); and *Contemporary Issues in Higher Education Law* (coedited with Kerry B. Melear and Joseph C. Beckham). His research has been cited by federal and state courts and has been cited twice before the US Supreme Court in writs of certiorari (once with Todd DeMitchell).